	DATE DUE		

Straight Talk About Parents

Straight Talk About Parents

Elizabeth A. Ryan

 Facts On File

Straight Talk About Parents

copyright © 1989 by Elizabeth A. Ryan

Library of Congress Cataloging-in-Publication Data

Ryan, Elizabeth A. (Elizabeth Anne), 1943-
  Straight talk about parents / Elizabeth A. Ryan
     p.   cm.
  Includes index.
  ISBN 0-8160-1526-0
  1. Teenagers—Family relationships—Juvenile literature.
2. Communication in the family—Juvenile literature.
3. Intergenerational relations—Juvenile literature.   I. Title.
HQ796.R93 1989
306.8'74—dc19   88-16530

British CIP data available on request

Printed in the United States of America
10 9 8 7 6 5 4 3

Contents

Acknowledgments

Many thanks to Dorienne Sorter, DSW, Adjunct Assistant Professor, New York University School of Social Work. Her generous advice was invaluable. Thanks also to Rachel Kranz, MA, for her contributions to the manuscript. A special debt of gratitude is also owed to James Warren, my editor, for his intelligent guidance and patience all along.

Straight Talk
About
Parents

1

Changing Families/ Changing Times

"**N**obody's family is as bad as mine!"

How often have you felt that way? Frustration with your family—especially with your parents—is a basic part of being a teenager. That's because the years between 12 and 20 are for most people a time of conflict and contradiction. These are the years during which you are figuring out how to break away from your family, how to develop your own values and lifestyle and identity. But these are also years during which, for most people, it's difficult to actually leave home. Besides the fact that it's hard for most teens to earn enough money to be self-supporting, you may also feel an emotional pull toward wanting to be taken care of by your parents—even while you are also wishing that they would just leave you alone!

When you were a child, you may simply have accepted your family without thinking about them. Even if you knew there were problems—a divorce, someone's drinking difficulty, a parent out of a job—you were limited by your age to doing little more than just wishing that things were different. Along with sensing whatever problems there may have been, you may also have felt secure in the knowledge that your parents were in charge and would take care of things.

Now that you are older, you may feel more rebellious. You have more experience in the world, so you have a better basis for comparing your family to other families. You are better able to imagine yourself as a grownup, living on your own, so you are more able to make criticisms of your family, thinking that when you are on your own *you'll* do it differently. Even if you love your family, you may wish to make some different decisions than your parents, brothers, or sisters made. Even if you agree with all of your family's values and attitudes, you may still feel frustrated, left out, or angry at times. And sometimes you may feel that *your* family is truly the worst family in the world.

Sorting out attitudes toward your family—especially your parents—is really a continuous process. Many grown men and women with children of their own still find themselves getting furious at a remark because "that's just what my mother always used to say!" or frightened over an action that they know "Daddy wouldn't allow." Because you both love your parents *and* wish they were different, attitudes toward them can be complicated and painful as well as loving and satisfying.

The good news is that there is a lot you can do to improve both your relations with your parents and your own feelings about your family:

You can find out more about families in general and how they work. That information will help you to decide how serious *your* conflicts with your family are. And it will help you feel less alone. The chances are good that no matter what you feel is a problem—or just a difference—about your family, somebody else's family has had the same problem or unusual feature. In fact, you may find out that *most* people's families are like yours. Or you may discover that, whether or not most people's families are like yours, many people *feel* that their families are different or "wrong" in some way. Getting this information may help you to separate "different" from "wrong," so that you can enjoy your family's special qualities while recognizing the problems that really exist.

You can learn a few more ways of communicating with your family. While communication is a two-way street, there's often a lot that one person can do to change the ways of talking and listening for both sides. One of the interesting parts of being a teenager is that you are finally old enough for your parents to start learning from *you*. Even if your parents don't realize it, they may learn to respond differently—and better—to your new ways of talking and listening (see chapter 5).

You can get in touch with your own conflicting feelings. No matter how bad an outside situation may be, you can always work on your own response to it. Being a teenager may mean having to put up with more control over your life than you'd like. Until you are old enough to earn your own living and establish your own home, the reality is that you will have to accept a certain amount of control and supervision from your parents. You may be able to make living at home a lot more pleasant . . . or maybe only a little. Either way, you can learn how to take responsibility for what you *can* control. Your parents may be able to control some parts of your behavior—such as by setting a curfew—but they can't control your response to it. Do you: Follow their rule? Get angry and slam the door? Try to talk things out? Bide your time while waiting to leave home? Find ways of getting into trouble to show how mad they've made you? Find ways to make the best of a bad situation? By learning more about your own feelings and behavior, you can at least choose your own response to a situation, rather than feel pushed into a response by your parents.

You can get help from outside the family. You may want another adult to talk to even if you are absolutely delighted with your immediate family and everyone in it. An older relative, a teacher, a counselor, a phone hot line, a mental health counseling service, or an adult friend may help you get a perspective on the people you live with. You may feel able to talk to this "outsider" about things you couldn't reveal to the relatives or step-relatives you live with. If you are seriously concerned about a family problem, particularly one that seems to be threatening, you should definitely find someone outside your family who can help you. If any adult is threatening your life, safety, or well-being, you have a right to get out of the situation. It may be difficult to find someone who can help you, but don't give up. For more information about especially difficult family situations, see chapter 8, "When Problems Can't Be Solved at

Home." For ideas on how to find another adult to talk to, whether you love or hate or don't believe you care about your family, see the directory at the end of the book.

This book can offer you some perspective on families—how they work, what other people's families are like, the problems and joys that families can create. And it can give you some concrete suggestions for how to talk to your parents, ways of talking and listening that can be helpful in working things out. This chapter will give you some more information on the many different types of families there are, and on how families have changed over the years. Knowing about different types of families may help you to put your own family situation into perspective.

Families Then and Now

Where did you get your idea of what a family is supposed to be? From television? From the first books you read in school? From your own family or the families on your block? Did you grow up thinking that most families were just like yours, or did you think there was a big difference between your family and the ones you though of as "normal" or "regular" families?

For many years in the United States, it was hard to find more than one image of the family. The "ideal" family as people saw it on television or read about it in their first-grade readers had a father, a mother, and at least two children. In this image, the father went to work, the mother stayed home, and all the children were happy to obey their parents. "Father Knows Best," the title of a television series, summed up this idea.

In fact, many families even in those days did not fit the pattern of the "normal" family. And the family itself has been changing ever since there have been families. Along with these changes in the family have come changes in people's ideas about teenagers. One hundred or even 50 years ago people had very different ideas about teenage rights, responsibilities, and capabilities than they do now.

For many years, there actually was no such thing as a teenager. Of course, that doesn't mean that there were no people on earth between the ages of 12 and 20! It means that these people were not considered a separate group. There were children, who required the care of parents and were too young to work, and there were adults, who could marry, work, and exercise other adult legal responsibilities. Young adults might remain under the care of their parents for many years. Although they might marry, for example, it would probably be a marriage arranged by their parents. They might continue to live and raise their own children in the home of their parents, and/ or to work for or with their parents on the family land or in the family business. Ironically, while these young adults in one sense seem to have had much more responsibility than today's teenagers, they may also have had far fewer choices.

Among the traces of this perhaps simpler time that many people still encounter today are such religious ceremonies as confirmation or bar mitzvah. These began as ceremonies of adulthood, marking the time when the child became an adult. Other cultures use similar rites of initiation to draw a clear line between dependent children and independent adults. Even though many people today still participate in these religious ceremonies, the ceremonies generally take place when the person is 13 or 14, hardly old enough to be considered an adult in today's society—though old enough to be married, have a trade, and participate in adult life hundreds of years ago.

Up until about 100 years ago, there was not really such a thing as a "teenager" or an adolescent (another word for teenager) in the United States. Various economic and cultural groups had different ages at which marriage and independence was considered acceptable. That age generally came earlier, at the lower end of the economic scale, as poor children grew up faster, married earlier, and got jobs sooner than the rich young people whose parents could afford to support them longer. But for all classes, there was general acceptance of the idea that parents' authority lasted until marriage, and sometimes beyond. Parental authority over daughters was even stronger than over sons, and an unmarried daughter, especially in a wealthy family, might never be considered independent. Many children from poor and working-class families did not expect to finish high school, or even junior high; only the very rich could send their children to college.

Also, there was very little sense of society's responsibility for children of any age. Children with living parents were considered their parents' responsibility, perhaps even their parents' property. If a parent wanted to keep a child out of school or put a child to work at a very young age, that was considered his or her right. Children without living parents or relatives were on their own. You may have heard of the Horatio Alger stories, which often featured boys of 13 or even younger living on the street, earning a few pennies shining shoes or running errands, until they gradually worked their way up to become well-off. The part about working their way up might have been a myth, but it was certainly true that in the middle of the 1800s, many children were living on their own in American cities. You can read about such children in English cities in the books of Charles Dickens.

For many reasons, attitudes began to change in the early 1900s. Social reformers like Jane Addams fought for the idea that society had a responsibility to protect children, inside or outside the family. As the types of available jobs changed, it also became more necessary for people to get an education. And with the rising number of immigrants coming into the country, schools were seen as a way to "Americanize" foreign-born children. For these and other reasons, laws began to be passed that both gave children some protection and limited, in a sense, their own and their families' "freedom." Child-labor laws forbade children below a certain age to work. Truancy laws required children below a certain age to attend school. Other laws were set up to protect children's health and safety in other ways. Gradually, the legal system began to distinguish between children and adults.

At about the same time, people began to come up with the idea of "adolescence," the theory that there was a special quality to the years between 12 and 20. Scientists and psychologists began to reason that physical and psychological changes take place during puberty as the child moves into the teen years. Of course, if a child became an adult as soon as he or she reached puberty, there would be no such thing as "adolescence." But, these thinkers asked, what happens if a child is physically old enough to marry but not psychologically ready, physically old enough to work but still in school preparing for a job? This in-between stage was seen as both physical (a time of changing hormones and physical characteristics) and psychological (a time of exploration and frustration). Teenagers were no longer children, but not yet adults; they had some responsibilities and physical abilities that matched those of older people, but were not yet allowed to take an adult place in the worlds of marriage, work, and other activities.

Does this picture of the teenage years sound familiar? If you had finished school at age 12, gone to work at age 13, and married at age 14, you would almost certainly have other problems, but you would not have the same "teenage" problems that you do now! If you feel "in-between" sometimes, it's because you *are* in between. That long stretch of time between childhood and the day of your first full-time job, your first setting up of your own household, may be filled with high school, college, vocational training, travel, internships, part-time work, responsibilities at home, and many different types of relationships and friendships. And of course, you no longer have to be married to set up your own household! In fact, for many reasons, society now offers many more alternatives to marriage than ever before. But whatever takes up your time and interest between childhood and the time you leave home, you probably sense that in-between feeling—no longer a child, not yet an adult.

Teenage Rights/Teenage Responsibilities

If you feel confused about where you fit into society, you're not alone! "Society" is also pretty confused, or at least contradictory. For some decisions, you are considered an "adult" at 18; for others, you have to be 21. For still others, you can be as young as 15 or 16, depending on what state you live in. For example, do you know what age you have to be in your state in order to:

- vote?
- drive a car?
- join the army?
- sign a legally
  binding contract?

- get married?
- drink?
- leave high school?
- work part-time?
- work full-time?

Deciding how or whether to make the above decisions is part of becoming an adult, yet there is no one single age at which you suddenly have all these rights.

By the same token, as a not-quite-adult, you have certain protections that society offers you. Do you know, until what age in your state:

- your parents are legally obligated to support you or to make some provisions for your care?
- the state will provide you with food, clothing, shelter, and an education if your parents are unable to do so?
- you are eligible for the juvenile justice system, which offers lighter and different penalties for most or all crimes, rather than being subject to the far harsher adult justice system?

And, along with its protections, the state has made some restrictions. We've already seen some of the decisions that have an age minimum. There are also some acts that are not "crimes" when an adult commits them, but are considered "crimes" if they are done by a teenager:

- staying out past curfew
- truancy, failing to attend school
- leaving home without your parents' or guardian's consent
- certain kinds of sexual relationships

So where do you fit into all this confusion?

Well, first, it helps to remember that however you look at these teenage years—whether you love them, hate them, or a little bit of both—sooner or later they will be over. At some point, you will be an adult, with a job and home of your own and with all the adult legal rights and responsibilities now enjoyed by your parents.

As you might be thinking, there are two sides to your status as a teenager. You might feel that the bad part is that you are presented with a set of mixed or confusing messages by society. Why, in some states, are you old enough to vote but not old enough to drink? How is it that you can earn some money at a part-time job but can't get anyone to trust you with better pay and a full-time job? You may also dislike the fact that your parents and other members of society—school officials and social workers—have more say over your life than they would if you were legally an adult. You may feel that you're ready to make your own decisions and you don't like other people telling you what to do.

On the other hand, hard as it may be to remember sometimes, there can also be a good side to being a teenager. After all, you don't have to earn your own living yet, or take full responsibility for running a household. Even if you are helping out at home financially and with chores, there is probably still someone else who bears the ultimate responsibility. The price you pay for not yet earning your own living is respecting the wishes of this other person—but what you get in exchange is some time to figure out what you'd like to do with your life, rather than being tied down with adult responsibilities right away. In the same way, schools and the justice system will make more allowances for you as a teenager than they will for you as an adult, in exchange for the greater restrictions that they impose.

In addition, if you feel that your parents or guardian are treating you in a dangerous or abusive fashion, you, as a teenager, are entitled to protection. Various types of laws restrict the kind of behavior your parents can commit and offer you various kinds of help and refuge. (For more information about this, see chapter 8.)

One hundred years ago, the law made no allowances for teenagers—and offered them no protection either. They were "free" to work long hours at low-paying jobs, to never get an education of any kind, to get along as best they could on the streets or on their own if their parents were dead or unable to look after them. Now teenagers face more restrictions—but more opportunities and protection, too. Teenagers are no longer so "free," but they are likewise no longer expected to earn their own livings starting at age 13. The freedom you have that these earlier teens did not have is the freedom to get an education, choose a career, and take some time to think about the kind of life you want to make for yourself. And again, whether you think this is a good trade-off or not, always remember: Sooner or later, your teen years will be over. You will have the right and the opportunity to leave your family if you choose. No matter how much you love your family, that's sometimes a good thing to remember!

More Than One Type of Family

Even 100 years ago, there were many different types of family in the United States. There were families:

- with a father who worked outside the home and a mother who didn't and a nurse who took care of the children;
- in which every member, from the grandparents down to the littlest child, worked together for the family farm or business;
- where the mother worked outside the home and the father was sick or disabled and stayed at home;
- where some of the members had been slaves, and so might have grown up without their own family members around them;
- that had lots of different kinds of relatives—aunts, cousins, nephews—living together, and maybe also a mother and a father, and maybe not;
- in which the mother, father, and oldest children worked and the younger children went to school;
- and many more!

And, of course, there were also families without children and families where children had many different parents, stepbrothers, and stepsisters. Even in those days, adults lived together in many different ways and for many different reasons.

Today you may know or belong to a family like one of the following:

- The father works outside the home, while the mother works at home taking care of the children (this is still many people's idea of a "normal" family, as reflected by the families in many books, movies, and television shows—even though statistics show that most people no longer live in this kind of family!).
- The mother and father are divorced. The child lives with one parent and visits the other, or takes turns living with both.
- The mother or father is raising children as a single parent because the other parent is dead, very sick, or absent for some other reason.
- Two men or two women are living together and raising children together.
- A child is raised by a mother and a stepfather, or a father and stepmother, or a mother and her boyfriend, or a father and his girlfriend, or some combination of all of the above! Various stepbrothers and stepsisters fit into the picture, too.
- Children live with aunts, uncles, grandparents, or other relatives and family friends.
- Children live with parents who adopted them, or with foster parents who care for them.
- Children change their living situation, living sometimes with a parent, sometimes with a relative.
- Some of the children live at home, while one or more child lives somewhere else: with another family, in a hospital or institution, with friends of the family.
- An older person—grandparent, aunt, uncle, family friend—lives with the family.
- The mother works outside the home to support the family while the father stays at home to raise the children.

Can you think of other types of family situations?

As you can see, there never was one "normal" type of family—whatever people may have thought—and there certainly isn't one now! Approximately one-fifth of all children in the United States now live with one parent. Since one out of every two marriages ends in divorce, this figure is likely to go up by the end of the century. Since most parents remarry fairly soon after a divorce (4/5 of men who divorce and 3/4 of women marry again within three years), many more kids are likely to put in some time with a stepfamily. With most women working outside the home at least part-time, and with some men choosing more flexible work and child-care arrangements, there are now many new patterns for parents. And since aging, illness, and physical handicaps have always been part of the human condition, many families include members that require of other members different kinds of responsibilities—"different," that is, from what some misguided people consider a "normal" family.

The fact is that every family has some ways in which it is like other families and some ways in which it is different. If you feel there is something "special," or "unusual," or "different" about your family, and if this sense of specialness bothers you, here are some things you might do:

Do some research. Find out just how many other families have a member who is blind, or a mother who lives in another state, or a parent out of work. You might be surprised to find out that you are not as different as you thought.

Find a support group. Often there are organizations for people whose families have special responsibilities, such as caring for a sick or handicapped member. Groups like Alateen and Nar-A-Teen provide help for teenagers whose parents or relatives have drinking or drug problems. Other kinds of groups may be available in your area. A support group offers you the chance to meet people whose situation is like yours. You get to talk about your good and bad feelings and find out how other people handle their situations. There are also support groups for kids who just feel frustrated or angry with their families, even if they can't quite name the problem. You can find a support group through the directory in the back of this book, through your school counselor, through a local mental health center, or possibly through your Yellow Pages. Organizations designed to help certain kinds of people—such as the elderly or the blind—may know of support groups that you can join, or may be interested in helping you start one. No problem seems as bad when you can talk about it with someone else who shares it.

Talk about your feelings with your family. If you feel, for example, that you are being given far more home responsibilities than your friends, because you are expected to care for a brother, sister, or other relative, you may not have to suffer in silence. You might talk to your parents about alternate arrangements that could be worked out: "If I agree to watch Chrissy on Saturday mornings, could someone else watch her after school so I can go out for the swim team?" Coming up with a reasonable plan, or presenting yourself as willing to discuss the problem, will probably be more helpful than simply complaining or losing your temper—and will certainly make you feel better than not saying anything at all.

Talk about your feelings with someone outside your family. If your family's situation is really unpleasant to you, and if you are not hopeful about working out a better arrangement with your parents, you might want to find someone else to talk to. A counselor, teacher, adult friend, hot line, or older relative might be able to help you sort out what can actually be changed in your situation and what you'll just have to put up with. If your problem is that your grandfather has to go to bed early, for example, you may not be able to play rock music as late as you would like, but perhaps an "outsider" adult can intervene to convince your parents that you really should have your own room to study in at night. In any case, talking to someone else can help you to sort out your own feelings.

One of the most important things you will do as a teenager is to figure out how you are like other people and how you are different. Everyone wants to be accepted, but everyone also wants to be just a little bit "special," too. Figuring out what you do and don't like about your family's specialness is part of growing up.

In the same way, almost everyone likes some things about his or her family and dislikes other things. Sometimes it's easy to feel embarrassed or ashamed at the ways in which your family is different or unpleasant—and then to feel nervous, guilty, or upset about feeling ashamed!

The important thing to remember is that your feelings are neither good nor bad, they just *are*. The trick is to use your feelings to figure out how you want to act. Is the thing you dislike about your family bad enough to make you want to change it, or are you willing to put up with it until you leave home? Are the things you like about your family good enough to make the compromises worthwhile? Can you find a way of enjoying the good parts of your family while trying to change the bad parts? Can you figure out what you can change and what you have to just accept?

These are tough questions no matter how old you are. Adults may have a very slight advantage when it comes to figuring these questions out—but only because they've been wrestling with them longer. If you can take on some of these tough questions when it comes to figuring out your feelings about your family, you'll have taken a big step on your way to becoming an adult. And, when the time comes, you'll find both leaving home *and* enjoying your family just that much easier.

2

Embarrassment and Shame

Has anything like the following ever happened to you? How did you feel about it?

You're all set to go out on a date. You've been getting ready for hours and you *think* you look great, but you're not sure. You come out into the living room and one of your parents says, "Hey, you'd better put a little more of that stuff on your skin. I wonder why your face looks so bad tonight."

You and some friends have made plans to go roller-skating. Your friends come over to pick you up. Your mother grills you for 10 minutes about whether the roller disco is safe, whether you might not break a leg, whether you will make sure to drive safely, whether you will be home by 9 P.M. Your friends hear every word.

You bring some friends back to your house for a snack after school. Your father, who is out of work, comes into the kitchen in his bathrobe, yawning and stretching. He has obviously just gotten up.

When your boyfriend comes to pick you up, your mother answers the door dressed in a miniskirt and tank top. She smiles and giggles and tells your boyfriend how cute he looks tonight.

You have just brought home your report card and, to tell the truth, you're not too pleased about it yourself. But that's nothing compared to how upset your father is. He looks at all those Cs and B-minuses and says, "Well, what do you expect? I never really thought you were the brightest kid in the world."

Parents do a lot of things—frequently unintentionally—to make teenagers feel embarrassed or ashamed. You might also have felt ashamed of your parents or your family situation simply because it was different from that of your friends. Coping with these feelings is part of learning how to accept yourself, your weaknesses as well as your strengths. It is also part of sorting out where you are similar to your family and where you are different. It may help to know that everyone feels embarrassed or ashamed about some things at least some of the time. It may also help to know that there are ways of coping with these feelings, both in terms of getting your parents to change some of the ways in which they treat you and in terms of changing some of your own responses.

Here are some of the ways in which you may feel that your parents cause you embarrassment or shame. As you read this list, think about whether any of these reasons apply to you. Then ask yourself what you can imagine yourself doing to change either the situation or your response to it:

You used to think your parents were the most wonderful people in the world. Now you realize that they have serious faults. You feel angry and betrayed, like they "tricked" you into thinking they were so great. And maybe you also wish those "good parents" would come back and take care of you.

Your parents tease you about having or not having a boyfriend or a girlfriend. Maybe you wish you could date but don't feel that anyone would go out with you—so your parents' reasoning reminds you of painful feelings. Maybe you don't want to date and feel that your parents' teasing is pressuring you. Maybe you are not sure of your feelings about the boyfriend or girlfriend that you do have, and your parents' teasing makes it harder to figure those feelings out because you feel like you have to defend yourself and the other person all the time. (All of these feelings may also relate to the teasing of a brother or sister.)

Your parents criticize you and pick on you a lot; it may even seem like they never say anything positive, only negative. Maybe they act surprised each time you don't get straight As or keep your room perfectly neat or win the trophy at the track meet—or worse, maybe they act surprised when you *do* do something great, like they've expected you to screw up. You may feel that nothing you do is ever good enough, or that your parents don't really expect you to be a very good person.

You do something that you are proud of—like getting a B on a tough science test—but your parents say, "Don't worry, next time you'll get an A." Even though they haven't criticized you, somehow you feel ashamed, as though nothing you do is good enough—and as though you can't even tell whether you're doing a good job or not.

You don't like the way your parents behave in front of your friends. Perhaps they treat you like a baby, or put you down. Perhaps they just aren't very nice to your friends, or maybe they're *too* nice, as though they think they're your age! You don't like feeling like a baby in front of your friends, and maybe you also worry that your friends are laughing at you or thinking less of you.

You feel that your family situation is very different from that of your friends. Maybe a parent or relative is out of work. Or you have less money or a smaller house. Or your parents have less prestigious jobs, or they live very different kinds of lives from those of your friends' parents, such as working at home or dressing very differently or spending their free time very differently. You find yourself wishing that your family was more like other people's. A divorce, an elderly relative, a handicapped family member, parents from another country or another part of the United States, or a family member with some kind of "reputation" in your school may be the source of some feelings of embarrassment or shame.

You know that your body is changing, often in ways that you don't expect or understand. If you're a girl, you are dealing or will be dealing with menstruation. If you're a boy, you are or will be dealing with wet dreams. These bodily functions embarrass or shame you, especially where parents, stepparents, brothers, or sisters are concerned.

Do any of these feelings sound familiar? Most people are taught that they're not "supposed" to be ashamed of their families, but, unfortunately, knowing that you're not supposed to feel something doesn't make the feeling go away. When people do something they think they're not supposed to do, they often feel "guilty," that is, they blame themselves and get mad at themselves for being "bad." Feeling guilty may be an appropriate feeling if you really have done something bad. But having feelings of anger or embarrassment about your family is not a reason to feel guilty.

Trying to hide a feeling, or pretending you don't have it, just adds guilt and fear on top of the painful feeling. You may feel guilty—mad at yourself—for feeling the way you do. Or you may feel frightened that someone will find out what an "awful" person you are. Neither of these feelings makes your original bad feeling go away. And both of them can make you feel paralyzed, unable to do anything.

If any of these situations ring a bell with you, relax! You can love your family and still struggle with feelings of embarrassment and shame. The thing to do is to figure out what you can change and what you have to accept, at least for the time being

How Your Parents Treat You

Strict parents may cause you embarrassment and shame in various ways. Perhaps they impose rules on you that are far more severe than those of your friends, such as a curfew an hour or two earlier, no dating or socializing during the week, or home chores that keep you from taking part in after-school activities. Perhaps they have such high standards for you that you feel like you are always failing. Whether or not you share their ideas about how you ought to act, it can be difficult to live with the weight of their expectations.

One way to deal with a strict parent is to try to negotiate on just one point at a time. If you start out challenging the parent's whole way of looking at the world—even if that's how you feel—you probably won't get very far. Saying something like, "None of my friends have to put up with all these silly rules—I wish you'd just let me do what I feel like!" isn't going to change this parent's mind, even if he or she is wrong.

Instead, try to psych out what is important to this parent and where the rules come from. If your school-night socializing is restricted because this parent is worried about you getting your homework done, acknowledge that this is a reasonable concern. Say something like, "I know you want me to get good grades and study hard—and that's important to me, too. Let me show you how many hours a day I'm already putting into schoolwork. During my study hall today, I finished my paper for history. This weekend I've blocked out all of Saturday morning to study for my math quiz. So you see, I am being responsible about studying. And, as a responsible person, I think I can afford to take the time to go out tonight." Keeping your negotiation to one small point—going out on one school night—gives you a better chance of success. Then, when you have won that point, you can come back later and say, "I went out last Wednesday and I still got a B+ on my math quiz. So how about letting me go out this Wednesday, too?" Perhaps you can change some of the overly strict rules gradually.

You may feel that you should not have to argue for your right to go out on a weeknight—and you may be right. You'll have to decide whether standing on principle and being right are more important to you than winning small points. Sometimes a small point is worth a lot of negotiation, sometimes not. You can't choose to make your parents less strict, but you can choose your response to that strictness.

As far as the embarrassment in front of your friends is concerned, it might help to state the problem up front. Say something like, "My parents are very strict and they make lots of stupid rules, but that's just the way they are and I've got to live with it. So don't say anything more, because you'll just make me feel worse." Being open about your feelings makes it harder for your friends to tease you about them. You can also engage them in your problem with you by asking about their feelings: "Do your parents do things that drive you crazy? Isn't it awful how parents can be so mean?"

If your parents' strictness takes the form of criticizing you when you fall short of their high expectations, it may be helpful to tell them how you feel. Instead of arguing or withdrawing, you might wait until you don't feel quite so angry or hurt about a criticism, and then say something like this: "I know you want me to get straight As, and believe me, I wouldn't mind that either. But when you make fun of me [or yell at me] about my poor grades, it makes me feel really low. I think I'd work better if you encouraged me more, instead of just telling me how bad I am. I care what you think. So when you tell me I'm no good, it really gets to me." Acknowledging your respect for your parents' opinions and letting them know that they are getting through to you might help them change their style. Sometimes parents feel they have to put things in the strongest possible terms because they don't believe that their kids are going to listen to them anyway. If you show your parents that they *are* getting through to you, they may not feel that they have to be so extreme.

You may also have to work on separating your ideas of yourself from your parents' ideas. One way to do this is to remember that your parents are people, too. They may be expecting a lot from you because they love you, because they are dissatisfied or ashamed of their own lives, because their parents expected a lot from them, because they genuinely do not understand your world and the pressures on you. To see the love, vulnerability, weakness, and fears in your parents' complaints can be painful. No one is ever *completely* ready to give up the idea of the all-powerful parents that we had when we were little. It can be scary acknowledging that your parents are unhappy, afraid, or unsure about something. But it can also be helpful to see that their criticisms and restrictions are reflections on *them*, not necessarily on you. It's tough to sort out constructive criticism from destructive nagging.

The more you focus on who *you* are and what *you* want, the easier it will be to see your parents in perspective, as people with fears, shames, and embarrassments of their own. That's because seeing your parents as all-powerful—whether all good or all bad—is often a way of running away from making your own decisions. All you have to do with an all-good parent is obey. All you have to do with an all-bad parent is disobey. Thinking about what *you* want will help move you away from your parents, and that distance will help you see them better. This "moving away" can be painful, but it does not have to mean that you no longer love or respect your parents, only that you see them differently. And that sometimes painful perspective is a part of growing up.

Overprotective parents can cause you shame and embarrassment in some of the same ways as strict parents. This type of parent may also have rules that seem foolish or extreme to you. This parent's expectations may also seem out of line with who you really are and what you can actually do.

Again, with overprotective parents as with strict ones, negotiate rules one point at a time. And negotiate in a way that acknowledges what is important to your parent. If you perceive that your parent is worried about some accident happening to you, acknowledge—even if they are overly worried—that he or she has a right to that fear. Don't just say, "Stop worrying, I can take care of myself!" Would that calm your fears if you were afraid for someone you cared about? Say, "I know that you're afraid I'm going to get in an auto accident. And I know that there *are* a lot of drunk drivers on the road late at night. But you know *I* won't be drinking. And I promise to drive defensively. I will be very aware every minute that there might be other drivers on the road who are not as careful as I am."

Of course, you are probably concerned that this negotiation take place in private, *not* in front of your friends! Perhaps you can make a deal with your parents: "I promise to abide by whatever rules we come up with—if you promise to talk to me about them in private *only*. I'll go over the rules with you *before* my friends arrive, or in the other room, if you promise not to say *anything* about our rules in front of my friends."

If you are not able to change your overprotective parents' behavior as much as you would like, once again you might engage your friends in the problem in order to cut down on the embarrassment you may feel in front of them. You might warn them before they come over, "Now when we get set to go out, my folks are going to go through a million little rules, so get ready. I'm going to stand there and take it because that's easier than fighting with them." Describing the situation ahead of time may make you feel more in control, rather than like a "baby" because your parents are worried.

Like overly strict parents, overprotective parents are often working out feelings about their own lives through expectations for their children. If you can separate your parents' weaknesses and false expectations from your own abilities and realistic expectations, you can relieve the sense of shame over not having done what your parents expected. Part of you may still be hoping that your parents will be completely and totally proud of everything you do. Or you may wish that just *once* they would praise you instead of telling you how you can do better the next time. Either way, try to get in touch with your own feelings and wishes. Even if you can't satisfy your wishes, it helps to know what they are and to say them to yourself. You may have to accept that some or all of your wishes for parental approval won't come true. But at least you can start to see the difference between them not fulfilling all your wishes for praise and your feeling like a failure. *You* haven't failed just because *they* haven't praised you.

Divorced parents may be a source of various kinds of shame or embarrassment for you. First, you may somehow feel ashamed or embarrassed about the fact of the divorce. You may feel that it somehow reflects on you that your parents no longer want to live together, particularly if one parent left home abruptly or is now out of touch.

For these feelings, it may help simply to remind yourself that your parents got divorced *for themselves*, not to do something *to you*. Feeling responsible for a parent's problems—for example, feeling that if you had been nicer to live with, your father wouldn't have left home—is often a way of covering up the real truth, that you had no control over the situation. It may be easier to feel guilty and embarrassed by pretending that you did something "wrong" than to accept the fact that your father would have done what he did no matter what you were like. Allow yourself to feel sad about your parents' divorce if that is how you feel. You may find that letting the sad or angry feelings surface gets rid of a lot of the embarrassment, shame, or guilt. Finding a support group through a counselor or through an organization like Parents Without Partners can be helpful here. Knowing an adult who has had experience with the children of divorce, or talking about these matters with other kids whose parents don't live together, may help you realize that, while there may be a lot to be sad or mad about, there's nothing to be ashamed of.

But perhaps your parents' divorce is causing you problems in other ways. Perhaps one side of the family is constantly critical of the other side: Your mother likes to tell you what a jerk your father is, or your grandmother tells you that your mother is an irresponsible woman. Either side of the family may point to events that actually took place in order to justify these criticisms, making you feel embarrassed or ashamed of the other parent.

You have several choices for coping with this kind of situation. You might try directly asking the other person not to badmouth one of your parents. Stating this wish simply and directly, rather than with anger and tears, may be most effective. This kind of request may make the other person uncomfortable, but perhaps being uncomfortable will cause the other person to stop! You may have to repeat your request more than once: "I know you and dad don't like each other, but it makes me really unhappy when you say bad things about him to me," or "You and I have so much to talk about—let's talk about something else." You'll probably find it more effective to have just one sentence that you repeat, quietly and calmly, rather than getting into an argument. After all, you don't want to win an argument that will involve hearing all of the other person's reasons for criticizing your parents—even if you get to answer them. You just want the criticism to stop. You can't change how other people think about your parents, but you can try to change what they say in front of you.

If you are not able to stop the criticisms, try to find a way to withdraw when they are being made. If possible, leave the room, or try to change the subject. If you are a captive audience, such as at a big family dinner, you may be able to leave the room temporarily, for example, by going to the bathroom—perhaps the conversation will be over by the time you return. The one thing you do not want to do is get into an argument defending your parent. If the other person is so committed to criticizing your parent that he or she can't agree to your request to change the subject, you are not going to convince that person of anything. And arguing will only give the person a chance to criticize your parent more. Remind yourself that the other person is making criticisms for his or her own reasons, not because your parent is a bad person or because you are a bad person for letting the criticisms go on. If you do feel the need to express your anger, focus on wanting the other person to stop criticizing the parent, not on your defending the parent. "He's my dad and I love him!" is much harder to answer than, "Let me tell you why he was right to do what he did."

Sometimes parents who are separated, divorced, or simply fighting can put you in the embarrassing position of being in the middle. They may "bribe" you with gifts or privileges, pump you for information about the other parent, or try to engage you in "reasonable" conversations about which parent you prefer or what is wrong with the other parent. You may go along with the conversation, only to find yourself feeling embarrassed or ashamed afterwards. If so, make a rule for yourself: Keep your relationship with one parent separate from your relationship with the other. Don't discuss *anything* about one parent with the other, even to answer a "simple" question like, "Does Daddy let you stay up as late as this?" or "How does your mother seem? Is she happy?" You have a right to the love of both your parents, and you have the right to be free of their conflicts about each other. When one parent asks something about the other, simply say, "You can ask Mom about that. Right now I'm with you—let's talk about *you*." You don't have to explain that you feel funny or ask your parent to change his or her behavior ("Please stop asking me about Dad!"). Just focus on how much you want to enjoy the time with the parent you are with. Even if your parents have trouble accepting that you love them both, you can work on having a separate and loving relationship with each parent.

Sometimes the children of *single parents* have difficulty accepting their parents' social lives. You may feel embarrassed or ashamed that your mother is going out on a date or that your father has a new girlfriend.

Again, these feelings may be covering up different feelings that are harder to face than embarrassment or shame. Are you afraid that your parent may like someone else better than you? Are you afraid that your parent will love the other person so much that there won't be any time or emotion left over for you? Are you worried that you might get to like the new boyfriend or girlfriend, only to have this relationship break up the way your parents' marriage did?

Coping with these feelings may still be painful, but at least you're dealing with the real feelings, not with the embarrassment or shame that cover them up. There may be some truth to your fears. Perhaps your mother *is* spending less time with you now that she has a new boyfriend. Perhaps your father *will* break up with his girlfriend and you will have yet another loss to cope with. Try to separate out the real from the unreal fears. Just because your mother is preoccupied now, does that mean she will ignore you forever? It's true that she has cut down on some special time with you, but has she cut down on *all* your private time together?

Likewise, try to separate out what you can change about the situation and what you can't. Perhaps telling your mother how you feel can lead to a new agreement. For example, you might agree on a special time each week that is just for the two of you to share. Of course, you're more likely to get somewhere if you are honest with her about your feelings ("I miss you and wish we could have some time together") rather than if you simply get angry or play upon her guilt ("I hate you! You're a terrible mother! You're always busy!"). Likewise, you might explain to your father that you worry about all the comings and goings of the grownups in your life. He may not be able to promise you that his new girlfriend will be in your life forever, but he may be able to reassure you that *he* will always be there for you.

Even if you can't change the situation to your satisfaction, getting in touch with your true feelings is better than covering those feelings with embarrassment and shame. If you don't like your mother dating because you feel that she has better luck than you do, you can at least realize that *her* activities are not the cause of your own painful fears. If you don't like your father having a girlfriend because it means you don't get to spend enough time with him, acknowledge that you miss your father and wish he wanted to spend more time with you. That may hurt—but it's better than blaming yourself or feeling ashamed of him.

How Your Parents Treat Your Friends

Your parents can treat your friends in many ways that you might not like. And your dislike can come out as embarrassment or shame. You may perceive that your parents are:

- flirting with your friends
- yelling at your friends
- teasing your friends
- criticizing your friends
- asking your friends embarrassing or personal questions
- telling your friends private information about you or your family
- revealing private information about your family by fighting in front of your friends

Here again, a good way to cope with your feelings is to begin by sorting out those feelings from reality. How much of what is going on bothers you because it is genuinely unpleasant to your friends? How much bothers you because it gives your friends information about you? How much bothers you because it gives your friends information about your parents? If your friends have this information, will they really think less or differently about you? Even if your friends hate or look down on your parents, will that affect how they feel about *you*?

Everyone wants to be proud of his or her parents, and to have friends look up to them. Sometimes this wish can be satisfied, sometimes not. It may be that your wish to have your friends admire your parents is so strong that you don't give either your friends or your parents enough credit. The fact that your mother mispronounced a word or that your father's new haircut really does look terrible probably isn't enough to make your friends look down on them—even though *you* might wish your parents could always put on a perfect face to the outside world.

Or it may be that your friends really are looking down on your parents, for good or bad reasons. Perhaps your friends have a hard time dealing with a parent's handicap, economic difficulty, or just plain human weakness. If so, you'll have to decide how this makes you feel about your friend, but you'll also have to work on accepting your parent's right to have problems and difficulties, just like every other human being. You may wish your parents were perfect, but you'll have to learn to accept them as they are—just as you want them to accept you, faults and all.

Perhaps, though, your parents genuinely are behaving badly where your friends are concerned. Some parents are very possessive of their children. They discourage their children from bringing friends home by being rude or critical of these friends. In that case, you can try negotiating with your parents. Try to find out what is really bothering them. If they are worried that you seem to be "growing up too fast," perhaps they just need to know that you still love and need them, no matter how many friends you have. If they are concerned that you are picking the "wrong" friends, see if they would appreciate a chance to get to know a friend a little better. Or perhaps you are just as happy that your friends are quite different from, even un- acceptable to, your parents. This can be a way of discovering your own values and opinions. In that case, accept the distance between your parents and your friends and try to minimize the situations where conflict can occur. See your friends away from home. Or share the problem with them up front: "My parents may be kind of rude to you. I don't like it, but that's the way they are. Let's just say hi to them and then go on up to my room." You don't have to apologize for either your friends or your parents.

An alcoholic parent, a parent who flirts wildly with a child's friend, or parents who fight openly in front of other people can make for difficult situations. If your parents' behavior is genuinely inappropriate, try to remember that *their* behavior is not *your* responsibility. Your friends, however, will react less to your parents themselves than to how *you* handle the situation. If you fold up in embarrassment, chances are your friends will be embarrassed, too. The unpleasant feelings all around might indeed make your friends uncomfortable in a way that will carry over to how they treat you. If, however, you give them cues for how to deal with the situation, your friends will probably be happy to come through for you. Telling them about the problem ahead of time, or right afterward, makes things easier. "You should know that my parents are fighting a lot right now," you might say. "I hate it, but that's the way it is, so don't be surprised. If they really start yelling, let's just sneak out and go for a walk until things calm down."

Or you might take charge at the time: When your parents start fighting, tell your friend, "Let's get out of here," and then, away from your home, say briefly, "My parents aren't getting along too well. I hope you know that blowup had nothing to do with you." If you feel like sharing your feelings with your friend, it might bring you closer. If you prefer not to discuss your family any further, your friend will probably respect your privacy. Either way, they will be comfortable with *you* no matter how they feel about your parents—and that's what you have to focus on. You can't control how your parents treat your friends, but you can control how *you* treat your friends.

If you feel that a parent or family member has a serious problem that is greatly affecting the quality of your family life—whether that problem has to do with drugs, drinking, or what seems like an excessive amount of fighting and punishment—you should contact someone outside the family to get help. Organizations like Alateen and Nar-A-Teen will not intervene with your family, but they will help you figure out how to deal with a difficult parent. You may also wish to find someone who can intervene in your family if you are genuinely worried for yourself, another parent, or a brother or sister. See chapter 6 and the directory at the back of the book for ways of getting help when your parents' problems go beyond simply causing you discomfort.

Coping With Embarrassment About Physical Changes

As you are finding out, the teenage years are a time of fast, uneven, and confusing physical changes. Pubic hair, hair growing on other parts of the body, development of the genitals, and the awakening of strong sexual feelings are common to both boys and girls—although these changes may not all happen at once or in the same order for everybody. At this time, girls are also beginning to menstruate and to develop breasts. Boys begin to have wet dreams, to grow facial hair, and to hear their voices change. These changes go along with strong and conflicting emotions that are partly caused by the hormonal changes and imbalances and partly caused by the social changes that result from looking and being treated differently.

These changes would be difficult enough to cope with if they only happened privately, but many of them happen in plain sight! This leaves the teenager open to teasing and possibly criticism and other kinds of mixed messages from parents, brothers, sisters, and other relatives.

How can you cope with such teasing? One way is to confront the person directly by saying something like, "Excuse me, I don't understand what the joke is here. Explain it to me, because I don't see anything funny." You may not "win" an argument, but you might make the other person uncomfortable enough to stop teasing you.

You might also want to have a private talk with one or both of your parents about your feelings and how you would like them to respect you. If your father is teasing you about your "baby fat," for example, you might find a time when you are not feeling too angry or hurt, take him aside, and say, "Dad, I know you don't mean anything by it, but when you tease me, I feel funny. I know you don't mean to make me feel bad, but you do." If your mother is constantly comparing you to "when I was your age," you might ask her to tell you more about what it was like for her when she was a teenager. Perhaps you'll learn something interesting—and stop the comparisons between her and you, which is what is really upsetting you.

Meanwhile, get all the information you can on what is happening to you and your body. You can check the resource directory in the back of this book, talk to a counselor, a school health teacher, a gym teacher, a minister, priest, or rabbi, or anyone else you feel comfortable with. You will probably want to talk about both physical and psychological changes, and you may want to find different adults to discuss different topics with. Your family doctor, for example, may be helpful in understanding physical changes, while a counselor at Planned Parenthood or a local teen center might be good for figuring out your feelings and how to handle them. And of course, you can always talk to your parents! You may be surprised at how helpful they can be if you come to them honestly with what's bothering you.

If you are embarrassed or ashamed about feelings you have for someone of the same sex as yourself, relax. Some people have sexual feelings for those of the same sex at some time or another, and these feelings are most common during the teenage years. Likewise, some people have had one or two sexual experiences with people of the same sex. You can use these feelings or experiences to decide for yourself what to do next. Most people end up relating sexually only to people of the opposite sex; some end up relating only to people of the same sex; some end up relating to people of both sexes. You may be able to find a counselor or support group that can help you sort through these feelings if they are painful or upsetting to you. This is a tricky issue because most adults have very strong feelings about it. Remember that there is nothing wrong with any *feeling* that you might have, and that how you want to act on those feelings is *your* decision.

Some Things That You Can Do to Cope With Embarrassment and Shame from Your Family

- Make a joke.
- Tease the other person back good-naturedly.
- Quietly and calmly tell the other person to stop.
- Get mad.
- Leave the room.
- At a calmer time, ask your parents about times that they felt embarrassed or ashamed. You might learn something useful.
- Write down your feelings or draw a picture of them.
- Find a friend, a group, or an adult to talk to.
- Remember that someday you will be old enough to leave home if you want to.
- Remember that your parents are people, too. Nobody's perfect!

3

Freedom and Privacy

Perhaps the most basic challenge teenagers face in coping with their parents is achieving independence. Dr. Dorienne Sorter, a school counselor and psychotherapist, puts it this way: Teenage is the time to complete the "widening circle of independence."

On the one hand, says Dr. Sorter, you're trying to develop confidence in your own judgment by trying out different ways of acting, thinking, dressing. You are looking for ways of life that will suit you best and that you have chosen for yourself, rather than simply accepted from your family.

On the other hand, there are your parents—and perhaps other adults—who for the last 12 or more years have been primarily responsible for you. They're probably finding it hard to give up the roles of advice-giver and caretaker. Now that you're beginning to try out different activities on your own, you may find your parents' concern oppressive, even "smothering." But think back a minute to what it must have been like for your parents when you were born. At that time, you were totally dependent on an adult. Whoever took care of you had to anticipate your every need; you couldn't even explain that you'd rather have a hug instead of food, or that you were crying because you were cold, not because you needed to be burped. The adults taking care of you had to feel their way to knowledge about what you wanted. As you got older and more independent, they had to keep you from doing foolish or dangerous things, like putting your hand on a hot stove or running across a busy street.

What's difficult for you about these teenage years is that you feel ready to try things out on your own—and you may feel that your parents won't let you. But what's difficult for your parents is that, once upon a time, if they had let you try things out on your own, you really might have gotten hurt. If they had waited until you *asked* for help, you really might not have gotten whatever you needed. Now, of course, that's no longer true, but it may be hard for them to adjust to this new situation.

And of course, as long as you are still in school and living at home, you really are dependent upon your parents in some ways, at least financially. As a young person, too, you still sometimes need the help and guidance that only an older, more experienced person can provide. It may be hard for you to put together the contradictory feelings: One day, you're an adult, ready to take on the world by yourself; the next day, you feel hurt and vulnerable and just want someone to take care of you.

In this atmosphere, it's possible for everything to become a battleground—what to wear, what to eat, what time to come home. Every detail of your life can become a test of your independence from your parents, your chance to prove that you really *don't* need them, that you really *can* make it on your own. This wish for freedom often leads to fierce anger against your parents. No matter how much you love them, it can sometimes seem that they are the only barrier standing between you and independence.

Ironically, the more angry you are at your parents, the more tied you are to them. Think about the last time you got angry at someone, whether your parents or someone else. Did that anger free you to go off and do what *you* wanted to do? Or did you find yourself constantly thinking about the person at whom you were angry? "I'll show him! I bet he thinks I'm wrong about this, but if I told him this or did that, then he'd see that he was the one who was wrong . . ." Instead of pushing the other person away from you, anger at him or her only brought the other person closer, deep into your thoughts and feelings. One of the ways you can tell that your parents are still very important people in your life is by how often you are angry with them.

This anger, and the fighting that goes with it, is a necessary part of life. "Arguing helps you sort out your own values," Dr. Sorter points out. "Kids need something to bounce up against in their search for self-definition." The trick is to find ways of fighting that are *productive*, that actually help you to make the decisions that you want to make, rather than lock you into a cycle of anger, acting-out, and guilt that only makes you more dependent on your parents.

For example, let's say there is a rock concert an hour's drive away from where you live. Some of the kids you know are planning to go. You think you might like to join them, but you also know that there will be a lot of drinking and drugs and the ride back might not be safe. You are faced with a choice that is difficult to *you*, one that requires you to make several independent kinds of judgment: Will you have a good time at the event or will you be uncomfortable there? Can you get safe transportation there and back or don't you trust the people who are giving you a ride? Can you afford the high price of the tickets, or would you rather save your money for that leather jacket you've been wanting? As an independent person, you have to choose among the pros and cons to make the decision.

Whether or not your parents would agree with the decision you made, you know there are definitely ways to present it to them that are sure to cause a fight. If you come in and casually announce your intention to attend the concert, making sure to drop in all the information that is going to most upset your parents, you are well on your way to guaranteeing a battle. This fight might help you to "make up your own mind": The more your parents say you can't go, the more you decide that you really want to. Your own concerns about safety, money, and whether you'll even have a good time can get swept under the rug while you focus on your rage at your parents.

Let's say that your parents finally forbid you to go to the concert—a decision you might have made on your own anyway. But because of the way you helped to create a fight, you'll never know what you might have chosen if the argument with your parents hadn't taken place. And you won't know whether, if you had presented your case differently . . . "Let me tell you about all the problems I foresee about this concert and how I plan to solve them. One: the driver of the car I'm going in doesn't drink or do drugs, so I know the ride back will be safe. Two: I've saved the money for the ticket from my after-school job, so I can pay for it myself." . . . your parents might have accepted your decision after all.

Instead, your parents have forbidden you to attend the concert, which makes you even madder than you were when you were fighting with them. Now you've completely forgotten your original wish to be independent, to make your own decision about whether or not to attend the concert. All you can think about is how angry you are with your parents. You spend the whole day of the concert letting them know in every possible way that you are furious with them. Finally, that night, although you don't attend the concert, you do stay out until two in the morning, just to prove you can. Your parents, worn out after a whole day of little arguments, ground you for a week.

Now you may feel guilty for having been so nasty to your parents all day, and for having caused them so much worry about staying out so late. You've "acted out"—done something you didn't really want to do in the first place—by staying out till two in the morning, just to prove you could. And you have new reasons for being angry with your parents; after all, they've just grounded you for a week! Instead of achieving independence, you've only proven how important your parents' opinions and actions are to you. What *you* really wanted got lost in the shuffle.

Think about all the choices that the *you* in this story *didn't* make. First, you could have thought through the original decision—whether or not to attend the concert—on your own, or talked it over with friends, brothers, or sisters, anyone whose opinion doesn't have as much power over you as your parents'. It's very difficult to discuss something with someone when you're not quite sure whether you want help from the other person in figuring out your feelings, or whether you're trying to win the person over to your point of view. If you are still trying to make up your own mind, you don't want to talk to someone who has the power to tell you what to do—unless you go into the conversation willing to accept that person's decision. The other person in the conversation needs to know whether you are saying, "I want to know what you think so I can do it," or, "I want to know what you think so I can go off and do what *I* want—but thanks for your opinion." If your parents let you make your own decisions about something, then it may be all right to discuss that topic with them, because both sides understand that the final decision is yours. But if you believe that your parents will want the final decision about something, don't go to them about it until your own feelings are clear to you—unless you are willing to let them make the decision for you.

So let's say you work your decision out on your own, maybe with the help of a friend or some adult who is not your parent. After all, working out decisions "on your own" or with the help that you get for yourself is part of becoming independent. And let's say that you decide that you want to attend the concert.

The next step is to try to accept your dependence on your parents.

Accept your dependence? In order to be independent?

That's right. If you go into the conversation angry and upset that your parents have the power to say "yes" or "no" to you, you're going to lose sight of your goal. As an independent person, you might later decide, if the concert is important enough to you, to attend it without your parents' permission, but you'll do it with your eyes open, knowing that there will be consequences to that decision. You won't act in blind anger, furious that your parents will probably punish you; instead, you will think clearly about what the punishment is likely to be or whether attending the concert is worth it.

As you probably know, making decisions is something that adults have to do all the time. Have you ever heard one of your parents say something like, "I don't really want to go to this party, but the Hodges' feelings will be hurt if we don't go?" They have decided that avoiding the party doesn't mean as much to them as protecting someone else's feelings. Or, on the other hand, perhaps you've heard one of them say, "I know my boss doesn't want me to take the morning off, but I really need the time to get ready for our trip this weekend." Your parents understand that there *will* be unpleasant consequences to the decision, but they are willing to make it anyway.

So, ironically, if you accept the parts of you that are still *dependent* on your parents—the parts of you that still care what they think, want them to be happy, and have to follow their rules because you live at home—you can strengthen the parts of you that are becoming *independent* from your parents, the part of you that is willing to let them be unhappy so long as you get what you want, or the part of you that will be leaving home or be financially independent soon. Accepting your dependence on your parents means you begin the discussion about the rock concert with them calmly, not in anger. It means you accept that they are likely to have strong feelings on this subject and, instead of being angry that they have the power to disagree with you, you understand their possible fears and can explain to them why these fears aren't necessary. Instead of resenting that you have to ask their permission to go, you focus your energy on showing them that you understand their concerns and are respectful of them.

Of course, sometimes you may just be angry and want to express it—and that's necessary, too. Or you may feel that you really won't know what you think about something until you bounce your ideas off your parents, whether that takes the form of a fight or just a heated discussion! These kinds of conflict are part not just of being a teenager but of life at any age. Being aware of these patterns can help you pick your battles.

Some battles that might be worth having:

- what time you come in at night
- whether you are allowed to use the family car
- whether your parents can order you to do your homework or whether scheduling your schoolwork is your own responsibility

- how much control you have over the money you earn yourself or over the allowance your parents give you
- whether you are allowed to choose your own style of dress

Some battles that might not be worth having:

- what you plan to do in five years, after you've left home (Why do you have to convince your parents that your plans are better than theirs? Won't it be your decision anyway?)
- whether your parents are wrong for holding their political or religious beliefs (Shouldn't that be their decision?)
- whether you are wrong for holding your political or religious beliefs (Should that be your decision?)
- whether a third person that you both know was right or wrong in doing what he or she did (Since neither you nor your parents have any power to do anything about this other person's decisions, what does it matter if you disagree?)

The decisions on your first list might be worth fighting over because they will affect your daily life—whether or not you are allowed the measure of freedom that you desire. The decisions on the second list are no less important in your growth as a person; in fact, they may even be more important. What you need to decide is how important it is to fight with your parents over these decisions, rather than explore the questions through talking with friends or other adults. Of course, if you enjoy a good political discussion or dissection of a friend's motives with your parents, go ahead. But if you find that every topic is becoming a battleground, you might be a little more selective. Go ahead and have the fights that you can *only* have with your parents. But save the other kinds of fight for people from whom you are already independent.

Coping With Your Own Dependence

One of the most important things—and one of the hardest—to remember about being a teenager is that *everything changes*.

Today you're at the bottom of a pit of despair, tomorrow you're on top of the world, and neither feeling, intense as it may be at the time, is likely to last forever.

In the same way, one moment you may feel like an independent adult, all ready to present your wishes and decisions to your parents in a clear and responsible way, and the next moment all you want is for someone to tell you what to do and to take care of you.

One thing you can do to make it through these changing feelings is to learn to accept *all* the different feelings you have: anger, sadness, disappointment, loneliness, as well as happiness, pride, and self-confidence. Another thing you can do is to remember that your parents may have difficulty keeping up with your mood swings, too! "They might be acting protective just as you swing into your independent mode," comments Dr. Sorter. Or they may feel they're acceding to your wishes by staying out of your way when all you want is for them to notice how bad you're feeling—the way you wished they would when you were little.

Dr. Sorter suggests relying on your sense of humor to help you through these times. When you feel hurt and vulnerable or in need of some emotional "cuddling," take out that baby blanket you had when you were four! Or acknowledge these mood shifts to your parents and develop a code: A white scarf means "I'm handling it, I don't need your help," a red scarf means "I could use some advice or comfort." Even if you don't get this specific, you might find a joking way of letting your parents know that you want them to change the way they're treating you at the moment, rather than letting yourself express anger and impatience. Of course, there are times when only anger will do, because that's what you really feel. But if what you really want is a hug and a, "Don't worry, I have faith in you," you're more likely to get that if you find another way of asking rather than if you just get mad.

You might also acknowledge your changing feelings to your parents after the fact. The day after a bad mood, for example, you might say, "I know I was pretty mad the other day. I bet I was kind of a drag to be around. But I feel better today." You don't

have to apologize, just let your parents know that you realize your behavior had an impact on them. After all, if you had a friend who was in a bad mood all day, wouldn't you appreciate hearing from him or her that the bad mood had nothing to do with you, and that your friend understands that it might have been hard on you? Giving your parents that same recognition makes it easier for them to get through your hard times.

Dr. Sorter suggests calling "time out" with your parents. Find a time when you are *not* angry and explain, "When I go to my room and slam the door, I just want to be left alone." You and your parents may need to come to an agreement about times when each of you needs to be left alone—or about times when each of you needs to be able to reach the other. It may help your parents to hear you say, "We'll talk about this later," rather than just, "Leave me alone!" Likewise, it may help you to hear them say, "I need to talk about this with you, but it doesn't have to be now." If you can work out these signals when neither side is upset, they can go a long way toward cooling things off.

As Dr. Sorter points out, "Wanting to be independent and wanting to be taken care of aren't emotions that are special to adolescents. They are emotions that are with us all throughout life. You can even say to your parents, 'You feel the same way I do sometimes, don't you?'" You can also pay attention to the ways that your friends and their parents treat each other. You might find ideas for how you and your parents might handle something, or you might find out how much you like the way your parents treat you. Or both.

In any case, remember what Dr. Sorter says: Relationships between parents and children are often frustrating on both sides because, "each person is trying to get his or her own way." The independent part of you may be trying to find its own way. But the dependent part of you, afraid of disagreeing or departing form your parents, may be trying to "keep your parents with you" by bringing them over to your way.

You are probably already aware of the ways in which your parents want you to agree with them. It might help to get in touch with the ways in which you want your parents to agree with you. Accepting the differences between you and your

parents is part of becoming independent. As you grow up, you may choose friends and associates other than your parents who are more likely to share your values and style. Try to figure out the difference between having the freedom to do what you want and getting your parents to agree with or approve of everything you do.

Protecting Your Privacy

Here again, this important issue may seem like a double-edged sword, both to you and to your parents. On the one hand, you want to protect your privacy. On the other hand, realistically, you have to tell your parents something about your life, if only to get their signatures on your report card or to explain why they shouldn't wait on you for dinner on the night you have a late practice.

Your parents, too, face a contradiction. On the one hand, they may wish to respect your privacy as they would like you to respect theirs. On the other hand, they feel a certain responsibility for you and perhaps a fear, as well. These feelings don't necessarily mean that they don't trust you or don't think well of you. It means that they are used to having to think for you—remember, this was a reasonable response on their part when you were four, even if it isn't any more—and that it's hard for them to learn when or how to stop.

As with the issue of freedom and independence, the more you can accept your parents' rights, the better you will be able to protect your own. If you come home obviously drunk or give signs that you may be doing drugs, what do you *think* they are likely to do? If you are going to engage in behavior that you know they disapprove of, you will have to find some way of taking their feelings into account. You can be pretty sure they will be worried, angry, or disappointed—and you'll have to decide if it's worth it to you to live with that. You must also be ready to face the consequences of your actions, which may lead to violations of your privacy. Although many issues can be negotiated, some cannot; you'll have to decide which behavior you are willing to put off until you're living on your own. You

may also discover, as you feel more responsible for yourself, that you are more open to taking the advice and help of your parents. It can be reassuring to know you don't have to make the hard decisions alone.

Often the issue of privacy is not about your doing something that your parents might disapprove of. You may simply want a right to a private life that doesn't include them. You don't want them to search your room, or even to come into it without knocking—not because you're doing anything "wrong," but simply because, as a human being, you want your space respected.

If you can convey this message to your parents, you've made an important step in protecting your privacy. Dr. Sorter suggests that you say something like, "I stay out of your room, so I would appreciate you staying out of mine." Of course, then, you *do* have to stay out of their room! If you enjoy slipping into your parents' room to borrow your mother's blouse or your father's sweater, you'll have a hard time making a case that they should respect your possessions.

It's human nature to be curious, Dr. Sorter points out: "You wonder about your parents in their private time, it's natural for them to wonder about you in your private time. But this doesn't give either one of you the right to pry. It's important to communicate that you want your privacy respected—but, unfortunately, not all parents are going to comply." If, after trying to make your wishes known, you feel that your parents are still not willing to respect your space, you might try to find a space outside the home where you feel you have control. Depending on conditions at your school, a locker might be a place to keep some private possessions. A friend's house might be another place, or perhaps the house of a relative or adult friend would offer you someplace to keep your diary, memory box, or cherished photograph album. Once again, if you are using someone's else's space, you should respect it the way you want your own space respected, and not use it for any purpose of which that person might disapprove.

When it comes to privacy, children of single parents often face tugs in both directions. They may be more aware than other teens of their own wishes to know about their parent's private life, while at the same time they want to protect their own privacy. Or they may feel that the single parent is even more focused on the teen's life, so that the teen feels burdened by attention and emotional demands that formerly would have been shared by the other parent.

If you are in such a situation, try to remember to keep your parents' feelings in mind as well as your own. You don't do this, necessarily, so that you can do what your parents want, but so that you can deal with them more effectively. For example, if your mother seems overly concerned with your social life, your concern is how to protect your privacy, within reasonable limits. But you can choose several different tactics for doing so: getting angry each time the subject comes up, giving one-word answers, responding with questions or taunts about her social life, giving her some information but not all, discussing why you don't feel comfortable answering her questions, suggesting that the two of you decide together which topics are off-limits to both of you, figuring out special times for the two of you to spend together in an effort to honor your relationship while still preserving your privacy.

You can do any or all of these things. The point is to pick the ones that you think will achieve your goal, rather than simply to react to the situation out of a feeling of angry helplessness. If you think your mother's concern comes out of loneliness, your response might be one thing; if you think it comes out of mistrust of you, you might choose a different tactic.

Generally, if you tell your parents some things about your life, you will find it easier not to talk about the things you don't want to talk about. Communicating some things to your parents reassures them that you do care about them and take them into consideration. It also helps give them a picture of your life, even if not the most intimate parts of it. Both you and your parents probably want to retain a connection while also learning to make space between you. One good way to do this is to choose what you want to share with them about your life.

Sometimes, especially for children of single parents, you may feel either very interested in your parents' private lives, or burdened when they suddenly give you information that you would rather not have. It may be especially difficult dealing with the fact of your parents' dating various people.

To some extent, you may have to learn to live with a situation you don't like. Even if you don't like your parents' dating, do you want them to go out of their way to help you pretend that they are not doing so? Would you rather that they lied to you, or that they gave up something important that makes them happy? Even if those are your preferences, you may not be able to get your way in that matter. And you might not like what would happen if your parents really did let you become the *only* important person in their lives; the responsibility and demands on you would be enormous!

What you can do, however, is set some boundaries about what you do and don't have to know. Decide what you would rather not discuss and make this clear to your parents. Then, if they try again to bring up topics you find uncomfortable, find a simple sentence to repeat, like, "I'd rather not hear about that." Use that sentence calmly, with as little emotion as possible, and then find a way to change the subject, or, if that's not possible, to withdraw temporarily. Don't engage in an argument, especially if you feel that the topic is a heated one on both sides. Arguing is likely only to expose you to more information that you don't want to hear, as you and your parents try to convince each other of who is right.

Likewise, if your parents want their privacy respected, especially with regard to their social lives, you will have to find a way to learn to live with their rights. You might want to try to uncover the feelings behind your desire for information. Are you curious because you are afraid the parent will like the person he or she is dating better than you? Are you worried that suddenly a new person will be part of your life and you won't have any say over it? Are you missing time alone with your parent and asking questions about the person being dated as a way to let your parent know you're mad about being left out?

If you can find a way to communicate these feelings to your parents, that might give them a chance to respond to your emotional need, even if the situation you don't like stays the same.

Your parents may continue to date, or to lead other parts of their lives in ways you don't like, but they may also be able to give you the love, attention, or reassurance that you want. At least you will feel more comfortable knowing what the problem really is, rather than pinning all your anxiety on curiosity about someone else's private life.

As you continue to make friends, become romantically involved, and perhaps care for children of your own someday, issues of privacy will continue to be important and difficult. People who love each other need and want to know about each other's lives. They also need some emotional space of their own. Working out these boundaries is always difficult, and in most relationships you find yourself working out these issues over and over again as time goes on and people change. The practice you are getting dealing with your parents will help you enormously in all of your future close relationships.

One final note: Every person has the right to physical privacy. If you feel that your parents—or anyone else—is violating your right not to be touched where you don't want to be, or under circumstances that are not comfortable to you; or if you feel that others in your household have access to seeing you undressed, in the bathroom, or in any circumstance that you're not comfortable with, you have the right to do something about it. If there's someone in your household who can help you change the situation, tell that person. If not, find someone outside of your household—a teacher, counselor, relative, or adult friend. Explain the situation and your feelings about it. If you don't feel that the person you have told has responded satisfactorily, find another person to talk to. You have the right to take care of yourself. (For more information, see chapter 6.)

Some things you can do to protect your privacy and still be on good terms with your parents:

Ask them about their lives, especially about when they were your age or about their own ups and downs. This will help you to see them as people, not just as parents—and you might learn something about yourself as well. If you're asking them about *them,* that might lead to conversations you can enjoy, real dialogue where you can also reveal yourself without feeling that your privacy was violated.

Figure out what you can happily share with them and do so, even if it takes a little effort. Nothing drives parents crazy faster than not knowing *anything* about their kids' lives. It leaves them free to imagine the worst.

Respect their privacy as you would like them to respect yours. Even if they don't follow suit, you'll feel much better knowing where *you* draw the boundaries. Treating them as you want to be treated will make you feel more grown-up and independent, no matter how they actually act.

Find a project that is yours and take responsibility for it from start to finish. You might choose a project you can ask permission for, like cooking a family meal, or a project that you can do without telling anybody, like reorganizing the storeroom. You'll find that the sense of being in charge and in control goes a long way toward establishing you as an independent person in everyone's eyes. You might also choose a project that has nothing to do with your family, like writing a short story or volunteering on a local political campaign. The more you feel that you are independently working on projects that are important to you, that require effort and that yield satisfaction, the less you will care about your parents' opinions and restrictions.

Remember that parents are people, too. They have a right to fears, weaknesses, and imperfections—just as you do.

4

Daily Life

No matter how well or badly you and your parents are dealing with the "big issues" of freedom and privacy, you still have to make it through the "little issues" of daily life: chores, money, manners, homework, curfews, and just plain getting along together. These household issues will continue to be important to you for the rest of your life, particularly if you spend time living with other people after you leave home. So the practice you get working out these issues with your parents will be useful to you later on.

Of course, the difference between working on these issues with your parents and working on them with other people is that your parents do, finally, have the last word. Some parents are good about working out rules and chores that all members of the family can agree on. Other parents have very strict but clear rules. Yet other parents aren't clear about their rules at all, but may still be disappointed or upset if it turns out you haven't followed them! As with the other issues we've discussed, you should start by assessing the situation in your household, so that you can decide how best to deal with it.

You might start by asking yourself the following questions. You can answer them to yourself or, if you are feeling especially frustrated or confused about this area of your family life, you might want to write the answers down. Don't forget to write down the things you like as well as the things you don't like. Looking at what you have written will help you to get a clearer picture of what you do and don't like about your family. You may be either happier or angrier than you realize! And, having the situation down on paper in front of you will help you to think clearly about what you want to do about it.

- What are the rules in my family? List all the rules you can think of, both the ones that are spoken outright and the ones that nobody talks about but that you feel are rules. ("Wash up after yourself if you eat between meals." may be a spoken rule. "People have to be polite to Uncle Louie even if he's rude to them." may be an unspoken rule.)
- Which rules do I think are clear to everyone?
- Which rules do I think are not clear to everyone?
- What can I do to get the unclear rules to be more clear?
- Which rules do I think are fair?
- Which rules do I think are unfair or unnecessary?
- Which rule am I the *most* upset about?
- Does anyone else in the family feel upset about this rule?

- What are the punishments in my family? List both the punishments that are spoken ("If you break curfew, you're grounded for a week.") and the ones that are unspoken ("If you mess up the living room, Dad will get real quiet and hurt, like you've just insulted him.").
- Which punishments do I think are fair?
- Which punishments do I think are unfair?
- Does anyone else agree with me about what I think is unfair?
- What do I think might be a fair punishment that could replace an unfair one?
- Which punishment am I the *most* upset about?

- Which chores am I expected to do? Again, put down both the ones you are told to do and the ones you know someone will get mad about if you don't do them.

- What are the chores that everyone else is expected to do? And don't forget to list the little things that everyone just assumes your mother will do (buy new lightbulbs) or that your dad will do (give you a last-minute ride to school if you're late).
- Do I think this division of chores is fair or unfair?
- Which chores do I think should be shifted from one person to another?
- Is there a chore I would like to trade for another chore? Do I think the person doing the other chore would be willing to trade with me all or part of the time?

- How much money do I get each week? Each month?
- Where does that money come from? (Job, allowance, allowance in exchange for household chores, bank account that someone started for me, other.)
- Does anyone ever have enough money! Given a "no," am I basically satisfied or basically dissatisfied with the amount of money I'm getting?
- Are the other members of my household basically satisfied or basically dissatisfied with the money that they have to spend?
- How would I compare my relationship to money with that of other members in the household? (For example, all of us are pretty well satisfied; all of us are just barely scraping by; I perceive that other people seem to have a lot of money whereas I don't ever have any.)
- Do I honestly believe that my parents could afford to give me more money? What do I think are their reasons for not doing so? (They're worried about the future; they don't like what I want to spend money on; they want to keep all their money for themselves and not share any of it with me; they think they have less money than they really do. Some other reason?)

Once you've done all this writing and thinking, stop a minute and ask yourself how you feel. Are you surprised that things in your household are as fair as they are? Did you just find out that you've been unhappy about something for a while? Have you gotten some ideas for changes you'd like to make? Most people have both positive and negative feelings about their living situations, whether they are living with roommates, lovers, spouses, children, other relatives—or even alone. How do your feelings stack up? Try to notice each feeling and idea that comes to the surface. You might even want to jot down a note for each one. Some people have trouble remembering the good things, others have trouble admitting the bad. Writing down *all* your good, bad, and mixed feelings can help you get a clearer picture of how you really feel about your household, and what the situation there really is.

Once you've gotten a sense of your feelings, look at each of the four list groups—rules, punishments, chores, and money. Ask yourself what you'd *most* like to change about each one. You might take a pen or pencil of a different color and circle the thing that leaps out at you. Or maybe you'll find that there's nothing you'd really like to change; you'd just like to make the arrangement that you do have work better. In that case, write down what you don't like about the way the arrangement works and how you'd like it to be different. ("I don't mind doing the dishes every night—but my brother is supposed to set the table every night and he never does. So my mother always asks me to do it because he's never home. I'd like to see my brother do what he's supposed to do—or at least I don't want to have to do his job!" You might write something like that—or at least write a word or two that stands for that long thought!)

Now look at the things you've said you most want to change. How likely is it that these things can be changed? How important are they to you? Here are some thoughts on different types of rules that may be helpful to you as you think about the rules in your family.

Every household—and, in fact, every relationship—is based on rules of some kind. These rules may be spoken ("If you can't make a date, or be home for dinner on time, please call ahead and let me know.") or unspoken ("Jennie has called me three times so now it's probably my turn to call her." or "I let Mom borrow my sweater so she owes me a favor."). By itself the idea of rules is usually not a problem for people. Even people who hate the idea of being "tied down" or "bossed around" will agree that there are *some* things they expect of themselves and others, even if it's only that you call each other by first names, or "Dad," rather than saying "Mister" or "Milord!"

So the problems come not with the idea that there are rules, but when people can't agree about which rules are fair, or even which rules are in force. If you are expected to call home when you're late for dinner, but your mother stays out late and doesn't call, that may make it unclear about whether the rule is for everybody or just for you. If your father *says* it's all right for you to skip mowing the lawn but then acts hurt and angry with you all day, you can't tell whether the rule is, "I have to mow the lawn," or not.

Sometimes, too, there are problems when your parents think one set of rules is fair and you don't agree. The easiest types of rule to change are the ones that are simply mechanical. If the rule is that you do the dishes and your brother mows the lawn, it's probably pretty easy to switch those chores around, or to share them, or to work something else out.

The hardest types of rule to change are the ones that reflect someone's values. This type of rule is often, but not always, unspoken. If your parents believe that girls should work inside the house and boys outside, it may be more difficult to switch chores between boys and girls. If your parents believe that "good" children always eat every dinner at home with their families, or that families that don't eat dinner together every night will be doomed to unhappiness, it will probably be pretty difficult to get your parents to change the family rule that everyone must always be home in time for dinner.

So if you are dissatisfied with a family rule—spoken or unspoken—or with your family's division of chores, the first thing for you to do is try to figure out *why* your family has that rule. Is it left over from when the children were all little, like a rule that says "no eating in the living room"? In that case, it might be pretty easy to change just by pointing out that all the kids can now be trusted not to spill.

Perhaps there is a rule that comes out of your parents' fears of not being "good parents." A strict curfew may be such a rule.

Your parents may feel that it is their responsibility to keep you home every school night so that you can study and spend time with the family. In such a case, you might try some different options. Just arguing straight-on ("This is a dumb rule. It doesn't make any sense!") isn't likely to get you very far because it doesn't speak to the feeling that created the rule. On the other hand, you're also unlikely to get very far if you say, "I bet you think you'll be bad parents or something if you let us go out on school nights. Well, that's pretty silly." No one appreciates being told why they think something; usually, the more right you are, the less the other person will appreciate it. (Think about it. Aren't you the same way?)

What you can do, though, is to *show* your parents that the things they are worried about *are* being taken care of. This way you are speaking to their feelings, even though you aren't naming those feelings. For example, if you psych out your parents a little and decide that they have given you a strict curfew because they believe good parents make sure that their kids do their homework and good parents always know where their kids are at every moment, you might say something like this: "Folks, I'd really like to go over to Ellen's this evening. Her parents will be home, and we're planning to stay at her house, too. Probably we'll just sit around and listen to records and talk. I finished my history assignment in study hall today. I do have a test to study for, but I've saved some time for that this weekend. I don't have any other homework that I need to do tonight. I'll be back by ten, and if you want, I can call you just before I leave so that you'll know exactly when to expect me back."

A speech like that tells your parents that you share their concerns, or at least respect them. They will know where you are and what you will be doing. By telling them what you *are* going to do, you help relieve their fears about what you *might* do. By describing your plans for homework, you are letting them know that you are concerned about that area of your life and you are in charge of it. By offering to call them before you leave Ellen's, you are showing them that you respect their fears for your safety. You don't have to agree with *any* of the values that your parents have about homework, safety, or your private activities. But by showing them that you are aware of *their* values, you make it easier for them to change the rules.

Notice, too, that this speech didn't come right out and ask that the school-night curfew be completely lifted. You've asked to go out on just one school night. If you keep your part of the bargain and your parents see that they can be responsible parents and still let you go out, you can go through the same speech again the next time. You might find that the curfew has been lifted without anyone saying anything about it. Gradually, the old rule ("No socializing on school nights.") has been replaced by a new one ("You can go out if you tell us where you're going and when you'll be back."). Your parents may even continue to believe that they're still operating under the old rule, or they may acknowledge that they have changed their opinions. Either way, you are getting at least some of what you want.

In addition to understanding your parents' feelings and then speaking to those feelings, here are some other things you might try when trying to change the rules in your house:

Give your parents lots and lots of information. Tell them what you are doing, who you are going with, when you'll be back, why you're doing it this way and not that way, how you know it will be safe, and anything else you can think of. Your parents probably will find the information reassuring, which helps both of you get what you want.

Be extra polite for a whole month before asking for a major rule change. Being polite means being genuinely ready to compromise, not sarcastic and resentful. Do the chores you're supposed to do, and find one or two extra things to do each week as well. Remember to thank your parents for the things they do for you. Try to avoid fights by agreeing with whatever really won't make a difference to argue about. If your parents, brothers, or sisters become sarcastic about your unexpected behavior—which they probably will—just smile and say, "I'm trying out a new way of getting along" or "I'm sorry you feel that way." Being polite in this way may not bring you closer to your parents. But it might begin a cooling-off period that gives you *and* your parents a chance to start treating each other different-ly. If you hate the way it feels to be so polite all the time, you can always stop, but it's a strategy worth trying for at least a few weeks, just to see how it works. Then ask your parents to hear you out and not to say "no" right away—and make your request. You might get what you want, you might get turned down, you might get a compromise you can live with.

Remember, no one is always right or always wrong, neither you nor your parents. If you feel that you and your parents are constantly disagreeing—even if you feel that's their fault—try to think of things you *can* agree on. And think, also, about saving your fights for the important battles, that is, the ones you absolutely can't avoid without giving up something that you very much want to do. Refusing to argue with your parents about your beliefs and values will buy a little space between you that might give you the chance to figure out these parts of your life for yourself. In an issue of that kind, just say, "You might be right. I'll think about what you have to say." It may be that all your parents want is the satisfaction of hearing that their opinion is still important to you.

If it sounds hard to you to pretend to believe something that you don't believe—or, rather, to act as though you might someday agree with your parents when right now you are sure you'll never change your mind—you're right. It is hard to have disagreements with people you love. And it is hard when the things that are important to you are not equally important to and respected by the people you care about. In the same way, some of your parents' rules, while they may seem foolish or un-necessary to you, are their way of maintaining their right to their own feelings. If your parents say, for example, "We can't fall asleep at night until you come home," they may be irration-al. After all, *you* know there's nothing for them to worry about. But their irrational fears have a place just as *your* irrational feelings do.

Ideally, both teens and parents should find a way to make a place for *all* of each other's feelings, both the ones that "make sense" and the ones that don't. Even if you feel that your parents aren't making space for your feelings, try respecting theirs. It may not change the situation that you don't like (a strict curfew, an unreasonable rule), but it may make you feel more separate from your parents and less angry and upset about something you can't change. And, of course, as soon as you leave home or are earning your own living, you will be able to change the situation.

A caution: None of this is meant to suggest that you deny your own feelings or experiences in order to make your parents feel better. If they feel strongly that you should attend church, for example, and you have developed religious beliefs that make that a conflict for you, that is definitely an issue you'll have to work out now, whether you work it out by defying your parents, going along with them, or working out a compromise. If your parents insist on serving you meat and you've decided that you're a vegetarian, you might not choose to do something that you feel is wrong just to keep peace in the house. And a certain amount of fighting and disagreeing is part of any healthy relationship. Just work on choosing your battles, rather than allowing your parents to provoke you into fury every time they open their mouths.

Some things that you can do to get along better with your parents (even if you disagree with them about almost every-thing):

- Find something each of them is proud of and compliment them on it.
- Make a point of spending two hours a week with them doing something you both like, even if it's only watching television and talking during the commercials.
- Ask their opinion about something that you do not deeply disagree about (for example, helping you to choose between two different outfits, each of which would be fine with you to wear that day; or asking for an opinion on which route to take to get somewhere), just so you're not *always* disregarding their advice.

- Think of something you might do that would make their lives easier and then do it.
- Try to read the mood of the house.

Some things you can do to handle disagreements when you do disagree:

- Remember the difference between a disagreement where your parents have control over the consequences of your decision and one where they don't. They can ground you for breaking curfew but not for choosing a career they don't like.
- Say, "We can talk more about this another time," either to them or to yourself, to remind you and them of when an issue doesn't have to be settled immediately. Find ways to take time out or a cooling-off period instead of getting locked into a circular argument that leads nowhere.
- Remember that you don't have to act on your own decisions right away, either. Acting when you are angry with your parents is probably poor timing. Even if you make the very same decision tomorrow, when things have cooled off, you'll probably be glad you waited. That way you know you're doing something because you really want to, not just to defy your parents.
- Never do anything you don't really want to do just because you are angry and upset with your parents. It's not OK to hurt yourself just to spite your parents, no matter how wrong they are. Do things because *you* want to do them, not because they *don't want* you to do them. Otherwise, they're still controlling you. And you're the one who pays, not them.
- Learn to observe your own behavior. Are there ways you can tell when you're really angry or upset or not thinking clearly? Do you ever do things in those moods that you regret the next day? Notice the things you do that let you know how upset you are: slamming the door, feeling trapped, getting a pain in your stomach. When you notice these "danger signals," ask yourself what you might do that

you might regret. Then ask yourself, what will happen if I put off doing that until tomorrow?

Dr. Sorter points out, "It's not so easy to become aware of the state of mind you're in, but once you start, it gets easier." She advises, "Take time out to look at how you react: 'When my parents are angry, this is how I usually behave; when I get an F, this is what I usually do; when I'm happy, this is how I usually act.' The more you are able to look at yourself in this way, the better you get at it." And, she believes, the more control you have, the more likely you are to make the decisions that are right for you.

Taking Care of Yourself

For a variety of reasons, you might find yourself living in more than one household during the year. Make sure you have some private space in each household, even if it's only a dresser or a drawer in a desk. If you can keep some special possession in each household, you'll be better able to feel like you're at home there.

If you are living with only one parent or adult of the opposite sex, you should be especially sure you have your own bed, your own room, and a private space for dressing, undressing, and personal hygiene. You should also be sure that you do have contact with some adult of the same sex as your own—for the questions that you or your opposite-sex parent don't feel comfortable talking about. Look around for an adult relative, teacher, counselor, or friend with whom you feel comfortable. Or contact an organization like Parents Without Partners, or one of the other organizations listed in the back of this book.

In any case, make sure that you feel comfortable with the contacts you have with the adults in your life. Sometimes parents can turn to a child for the warmth and affection that they would normally get from another adult. This does not have to take the form of actual sexual activity in order to make you uncomfortable. Sometimes warmth and affection take on sexual overtones without this being intended—but, intentional or not, you may feel uneasy. Be sure that you have the physical space you need, and someone to talk to about your feelings. You are not betraying a parent by not feeling comfortable with everything he or she does. You are simply taking care of yourself, which, as you grow toward being an adult, is your responsibility.

Likewise, if you feel that you are being given too much emotional responsibility by your parents, find a way to let your parents know that you are still their child and that you are not yet ready to take on adult responsibilities in your household. Single-parent homes may be especially prone to encouraging one or more of the children to take the place of the missing adult.

For example, it's all right to let your parents share in your life. But if you feel that you are becoming your mother's "best friend" or your dad's "little wife," it may be time to set some limits. You have a right to parenting from your parents, but they should be finding "best friends" their own age, not turning to you for the advice and comfort that one usually gets from a friend. Likewise, they should have activities of their own, rather than being wrapped up completely in your life. You are not obligated to keep the adults in your family from feeling lonely or abandoned.

In the same way, you may have financial responsibilities at home. But, until you are out of high school, you aren't able to take adult responsibilities in a household and there's no reason why you should. If you find yourself worrying too much about money or feeling the burden of unpaid bills, let your parents know about the pressure you are feeling. Or find someone to talk to who can help you sort out how much responsibility it's appropriate for you to take. Your parents are supposed to take care of you. You aren't supposed to take care of *them*.

If you do feel that your parents aren't doing a good enough job of taking care of you, and if you feel that you've tried your best to work this out with them, you can try to change the situation. There are people out there who *can* help take care of you. Find them. A social service agency, counseling service, or support group like Parents Without Partners or Alateen may be able to help you find the adult support and advice that you are not getting at home. It is not betraying your parents for you to search for what you need.

Daily Life in Single-parent Homes and Stepfamilies

The rules of daily life may switch a good deal over the years. As households change and people grow, different rules become necessary as old rules become impractical. The teen living in a single-parent home or stepfamily may find him- or herself living with newly changed rules, or with more than one set of rules at a time.

It is hard to cope with changes in the routine of daily life, particularly changes that you didn't choose yourself. Ideally, you can find ways after a divorce or other change in family structure to widen your idea of who belongs in your family, even while you probably also feel the loss of a familiar pattern. But even if you can accept the idea of adding stepparents, brothers, and sisters to your family, you still have to find ways to live with all those people!

In these situations, especially, try to clarify the household rules. If you are living in what feels like "someone else's house," that is, a home where you and/or your parent are the newcomers to a preexisting set of rules and customs, you might focus first on finding out just what the rules are. The unspoken rules are the hardest ones to find out, of course. Because everyone takes them for granted, it doesn't occur to anyone to talk about them—until, of course, you've broken one by accident, causing anger or hurt feelings when you didn't mean to. Or it may be your feelings that are bruised as you discover that you're not going to be allowed to eat with the "grownups" at a dinner party, even though you always did "at home"; or that your favorite television program, that you've been looking forward to all week, is superseded by some adult's new preference for "Masterpiece Theater."

What you might do in a situation like this is to focus on *finding out* the spoken and the unspoken rules *without* judging them. When you feel yourself reacting to the new rules, remind yourself that you can decide anything you want to about these rules *later*. But first, you must want to find out what they are. This will help you to deal with your own feelings of loss and grief, which might at first make *any* change seem like a bad one, just because it's different. After you fully understand what the changes are, then you can decide whether you like them or not.

Focusing on finding out the rules also gives you a chance to learn more about the new household. You will be able to be sensitive to little things, like finding out that your stepmother gets very nervous each day before work, so the rule is, "Don't talk to her in the morning," or that your stepsister doesn't mind lending her socks but hates to share her sweaters. Of course, once you've found out these unspoken rules, you can choose not to go along with them or to try to change them. But at least you've found out what they were, rather than become overwhelmed by the changes.

Once you have found out the rules of the new household, you can use some of the same communications skills discussed earlier to try to make the rules more fair, more clear, or easier for you to live with. Likewise, if other members join *your* household, or if you and steprelatives form a new household together, you can be sensitive to other people's needs while still working to protect your own. Sometimes it helps to separate things, to say, "Now I'm only going to get information about so-and-so's feelings," "*Now* I'm going to focus on how *I* feel," and "Now I'm going to decide what to *do*." Just be sure you always leave room for your own feelings in whatever decision you come to.

Knowing your own feelings is essential in choosing the actions that will work best for you. That way, you can choose an action that you believe will satisfy your feelings, instead of just reacting impulsively. Putting your feelings together with a realistic assessment of your situation is the best way of making daily life run smoothly for everybody.

5

Communicating

Several years ago, the movie *Cool Hand Luke* made the following line popular: "What we have here is a failure to communicate."

Do you have a "failure to communicate" in your family? Do you feel that your parents just don't understand you, or worse, that they don't even listen to you? Do you ever feel that you just don't understand your parents, or that you would rather *not* listen to them?

Good communication means that you are talking so that the other person understands what you mean, and you are listening so that you understand what the other person means. Communication isn't just hearing somebody else's words. It's understanding what the other person means by those words. Sometimes that means getting your own assumptions, fears, or hopes out of the way.

Have you ever had these kinds of communication with your parents?

You: I'd like to borrow the car next weekend, OK?

Parent: We'll see. I might need the car myself on Saturday. Where do you want to go?

What You "Hear" Parent Saying:	I'm more important than you are, so why should I let you have the car when I might need it myself? Besides, I don't trust you. Where do you want to go, anyway? Probably someplace I don't approve of. There really isn't much chance I'll give you the car—or anything else you really care about.
You:	I've finished making dinner and the table is all set.
Parent:	That's great! You're always such a big help around the house.
What You "Hear" Parent Saying:	I expect you to help me all the time, so what you did this time doesn't count very much. Be careful not to slip. You're not allowed to be any other kind of person except a "big help around the house."
You:	I'm going to bed now.
Parent:	Good heavens, it's past midnight! I'd like to hear where you were out so late.
What you "Hear" Parent Saying:	I don't trust you to stay out late and I expect you to tell me everything you did so that I can check up on you. I'm sure that whatever you were doing, it was something bad.

As you can see, there are always two parts to every act of communication: speaking and listening. In the three examples given above, the parent *might* have meant what the teen thought. But isn't it possible that the parent really meant to communicate something else?

You:	I'd like to borrow the car next weekend, OK?
Parent:	We'll see. I might need the car myself on Saturday. Where do you want to go?
What Parent Wants to Communicate:	I wish I could say yes to you all the time, but I do have commitments of my own. Let me know how important your plans are to you and let's see what we can work out.
You:	I've finished making dinner and the table is all set.
Parent:	That's great! You're always such a big help around the house.
What Parent Wants to Communicate:	I appreciate what you just did and I want to let you know it, but of course, I would love you and appreciate you whether you helped around the house or not.
You:	I'm going to bed now.
Parent:	Good heavens, it's past midnight! I'd like to hear where you were out so late.
What Parent Wants to Communicate:	I care about you, so I am a little concerned when you're out late. Please reassure me that I have nothing to worry about so that I can go on trusting you and calm my own fears.

As you already know, communication can be a tricky business. From one person, "I love you" can sound like an insult.

Another person can say, "You jerk!" and make it sound like the most loving message in the world. When you are on the listening side of communication, how do you know what the other person really means?

Sometimes it may be pretty obvious. If your father is yelling at the top of his voice, probably he's angry. If your mother is drumming her fingers on the table and biting her lip, there's a good chance that she's nervous.

Even in these cases, however, your parents may be communicating more than what seems obvious. Is your father's anger coming out of his own fears about something, his worry for you, or even his own frustration with himself for not being a better parent? If you ask for an advance on your allowance and he blows up, is he saying that you're careless and irresponsible with money (which may be the words that he's using), or is he saying that he feels upset that he doesn't have more money to give you? If your mother seems nervous about you asking permission to stay out late, is it because she doesn't trust you or because she knows it's time to let you go out on your own a little and she can't help feeling sad about it?

As you can see, your own feelings, hopes, and assumptions play a big part in how you hear what the other person means to communicate. If you are sure that your parents don't trust you, everything they say is going to sound like lack of trust. If you are sure that your father won't let you borrow the car or your mother doesn't want to raise you allowance, anything they tell you about those issues may sound like what you already expected to hear.

Another interesting part of listening is that the way you listen can actually affect the person who is talking. Let's say that one of your parents says, "We'll see about you borrowing the car. Where do you want to go?" If you hear that as "I don't trust you" or "I don't care enough about you to lend you the car," what might you say back? Perhaps:

"You don't care about me, do you?"
"You never let me borrow the car."

"You never let me do anything I want."
"All you care about is yourself."
"I don't have to tell you where I'm going."
"Why do you always check up on me?"
"Can't you ever just say yes?"

What do you think your parents are likely to say in response to one of those statements? Is this a discussion that is likely to lead to your getting to borrow the car? Even if you do get to borrow the car, how are you and your parents likely to feel? A conversation like that could easily end up with parents angry because they are mistrusted and you more sure than ever that your parents don't trust you.

On the other hand, suppose you decide that your parent really means, "I trust you, but I have my own fears and concerns. Please tell me where you are going so that I can have a picture in my mind of you being safe and happy." If that is what you hear, your response might be quite different:

"My friend Ruth and I are going to the mall."
"I want to go for a drive with Joe and Petey—you remember, you met them last week. We'll drive carefully and be back by eleven."
"I've got a date. I'm not sure where we're going, but I'll fill the tank with gas before I come home."

These responses are based on the expectation that your parents want to say yes. They show that you are aware of your parents' possible concerns and that you care enough about your parents to respect those concerns (even if *you* know there's nothing to be concerned about). By assuming that your parents do trust you and do want to say yes, you've made replies that actually increase the chances of this being so.

That's the funny thing about expectations. People tend to do what we expect them to do. If you expect your parents to say no, to mistrust you, or to be angry with you, you are likely to hear everything they say as proof of what you expect. Then you're likely to answer not what your parents really said or meant to say, but only what you expected them to say. Answering based on your expectations may actually help those expectations come true. If your parents get the impression that you are expecting them to say no, they may decide that they really should say no. If they see that you are honestly expecting them to trust you, to care about you, and to say yes wherever possible and reasonable, they may actually meet those expectations!

You probably know how this works from being on the other side of it. Have you ever come home in a great mood only to find that a family member *expects* you to be in a bad mood? Nothing can ruin a good mood so quickly as someone saying in a surprised voice, "Well, *you're* certainly cheerful this afternoon!" On the other hand, if someone rushes up to you with a big smile and says, "I've got great news for you," you probably start to smile yourself and get set to be excited and pleased.

Of course, listening is still only one half of the conversation. If your parents are really communicating anger, mistrust, or a definite "no," you may just have to live with their reactions and decisions. But before you decide that the "same old thing" is happening again, ask yourself if you are really listening to them or to you? You might be surprised at what you find out!

Questions to ask yourself to help your listening:
1. Am I hearing this communication in the most negative possible way? Is there a more positive way I can hear this?
2. Am I making up my own interpretation of what's going on? If, for example, my parent is angry, am I clear on exactly what he or she is angry about? If my parent is nervous, am I clear on what would help him or her to feel less nervous?
3. Have I given up on having a pleasant conversation before the conversation has ever begun?
4. Am I letting my expectations get in the way of hearing what's really being said?
5. What can I do to help the other person be clear about what he or she is saying?

What about the other half of communication? How can you express yourself in such a way that your parents—and other family members—are clear about what you're saying?

Of course, sometimes you may feel that you don't *want* your parents to be clear on what you're saying. Many of us hold some beliefs that lead us to keep some thoughts or feelings to ourselves. Sometimes we believe that we "invented" these beliefs that are directly taught to us by our parents. Either way, they can get in the way of honest communication. Do any of these ideas sound familiar to you?

If I really told that person how angry I was, she (or he) wouldn't be able to take it. She'd be really hurt and she might not get over it. Believing that your anger is so powerful that it can hurt another person badly, perhaps even destroy that person, is a very frightening feeling. If you really had the power to destroy another person with your anger, it would make sense to hold that anger in at all costs. The problem is that, by holding in your anger, you hold in a lot of other feelings, too. And you don't give the other person a chance to respond to you. If you can find a constructive way to express your anger, when you feel it, you will probably find that you are in touch with a lot of other feelings as well. And you will certainly discover that your anger does not destroy another person, even if that person doesn't especially like your being angry.

If I really said what I felt, he (or she) would feel so bad. Being afraid that any of your feelings—sadness, anger, excitement over a new romance, a wish for more independence—will upset another person is likely to lead to your hiding those feelings. If you are afraid that honest communication will cause pain to someone you care about, you may feel that it's better not to be honest. Sometimes, of course, it's better to be tactful. "That new look really isn't my style." may be more appropriate than, "I hate that haircut!" But if you feel that you are hiding your feelings about something that is very important to you, you might consider what would *really* happen if you shared those feelings. Perhaps someone would "feel bad"—but only you can decide if that consequence means more to you than hiding your feelings.

I feel awful and it's all your fault! Blaming another person for how you feel can very easily get in the way of honest communication. If you begin a conversation with that attitude, the other person's chances of wanting to hear and understand you are much less. By beginning a conversation with blame, you are practically guaranteeing that the other person won't hear anything except that you think he or she is wrong. The other person will be so busy building a case in self-defense that the rest of *your* communication is likely to get lost.

If a person loves you, it's not necessary to tell him or her what's going on. The other person should "just know." The idea that another person can read your mind if he or she really cares about you is very deep-rooted in many people. It probably comes from being a baby, when your parents did in fact have to "read your mind." A baby can't ask for what it wants, so parents have to guess. What a child wants, however, is more complicated than a baby's simple demands of food, clothing, and being hugged. And what a teenager wants is even more complicated. At times, you're probably glad your parents can't read your mind any more! There may be other times, however, when you think they should be able to know that you're not talking to them because you're nervous about an exam or hurt at a rejection from a friend. You may wish they "just knew" why you're feeling bad—to the point where you feel angry about needing to put your feelings into words.

I tried talking to Dad (or Mom) last week and it didn't work, so why should I bother? Most of us tend to think that things will continue to be the way they've always been. If someone rejected us once, that person will probably continue to reject us forever. If someone frequently gets angry, asks embarrassing questions, or insists on rules that seem unreasonable, we should expect that this person's behavior will never change.

In some cases, this is true. Some people do not change their behavior, no matter what the people around them do. However, in some cases, if you change your behavior, your parents' behavior may also change. If you begin to communicate honestly and openly, you may find that they respond to you differently. It may not happen overnight. Your parents may also hold this belief about people not changing, to the point where they don't even notice that you *have* changed. (In fact, as a growing teenager, you may be feeling this way anyway!) Even if your parents' behavior doesn't change radically, though, you may find that changing *your* behavior does help you all to get along better. And you may find that *you* feel better communicating honestly, no matter how your parents respond.

I don't really know how I feel. When someone asks me, I go blank. If you hold this belief about yourself, you are likely to think that honest communication is impossible. How can you communicate with someone honestly about your feelings if you don't know what they are?

In fact, you may be hiding your feelings from yourself so that you don't have to share them with someone else. If you experience yourself as "going blank," ask yourself what that blankness is covering up. You might find that it helps to write some thoughts in a private journal, to draw pictures based upon your ideas, or just talk with someone you trust outside your family. As you try to express your feelings, to yourself or to others, you'll find that you become more and more aware of them. Then you have the choice about what you want to communicate to your family.

I'm just not the kind of person who shows a lot of emotion. I don't like to talk things to death. It's true that everyone has his or her own style of communication. Some people communicate more in words; others communicate in other ways. Whatever your style, though, you are always communicating *something*. Your silence may be communicating anger, indifference, nervousness, acceptance, or some other emotion—all without you realizing it. That's why taking responsibility for your communication—however you do it—is so important.

Nobody would listen to me anyway. It's true that there are limits to what you can accomplish by communicating your thoughts or feelings with your family. But deciding that you have absolutely no power to affect events puts you and everyone around you into a box with no way out. By deciding that no one will listen to you, you aren't giving anyone else a chance to do so. You also aren't taking any responsibility for getting what you want. Sometimes it can be easier to decide that no one will listen to you than to take a risk and make yourself heard—but it might be rewarding to take the risk.

Talking about myself is selfish. I'd rather hear what everyone else thinks. Listening to others and being concerned about what they think is a wonderful quality. If the "unselfish" person is bottling up his or her own thoughts and feelings, however, he or she is really taking something away from others. People who refuse to share their true thoughts and feelings are depriving others of the chance of really getting to know them and be close to them.

Why should I talk about anything with anybody? Whatever is going on, I can handle it by myself. Again, independence is a wonderful quality, and people who know they can take care of themselves can face the world with confidence and enthusiasm. But every human being has times of needing help, support, or just the chance to get thoughts and feelings out in the open. And by not communicating honestly with the people around you, you are depriving them of the chance to be involved in your life.

Communicating honestly and openly with your family can be scary, especially if you perceive that others in your family do not communicate that way. You may have fears about letting others know your true feelings, your opinions, or your wishes. You may also be able to see new possibilities in this type of communication. Here are some fears that many people have about communicating openly, along with some possibilities that this type of communication opens up.

Fears:
- I'll be criticized for my opinions.
- No one will like me if they know how I really feel.
- Everyone will just leave me alone when they find out what I think.
- Mom (or Dad, or some other family member) will really let me have it if they find out I think this way.
- No one could possibly understand why I feel this way.
- I'd feel bad making everyone else uncomfortable.

- The things that people would find out about me don't go with my image.
- Dad (or Mom, or some other family member) would really find a way to "get" me if I said what was on my mind.
- Once I say what I think, I'll be trapped. I'll have to think that way all the time, and what if I'm wrong, or change my mind?

Possibilities:
- Our family might find new ways of handling old problems.
- We might get closer.
- I might really clear the air of some things that have been bothering me—and others—for a while.
- I'd really get to understand how Mom (or Dad, or some other family member) feels.
- If I said what I felt and nothing bad happened, I might accept myself more easily.
- Maybe we'd all grow from this new experience.
- I could give more to other people in my family—and they could give more to me—if we knew each other better through this type of communication.
- I'd feel honest instead of like a fraud.
- I'd feel powerful saying what I thought and felt, and maybe others would feel that way too.
- It's good practice for future relationships.

Do the rewards seem worth the risks? Every family is different and only you can decide what kind of communication will work best between you and your family. Honest communication doesn't mean telling another person *everything*. Nor does it mean expecting the two of you never to disagree or to fight. What it does mean is choosing carefully what you want the other person to hear and then doing everything you can to make sure that the message you have chosen is getting across.

For example, let's say you want to go to a school dance and you want permission to stay out two hours later than usual. Your parents are concerned about your being out late. You may honestly think or feel that this is a ridiculous fear. It isn't necessarily being dishonest to keep this opinion to yourself. In fact, what will probably be more helpful to the communication you want is to let your parents know that you have heard what *they* are communicating. You can do this without expressing your opinion about it:

Parents: Oh, my God! You want to stay out till *when*?

You: I understand that you're nervous about my staying out late.

Parents: You'd better believe we're nervous! Are you crazy?

You: I know you're concerned about me being safe. Let me tell you how I'm taking care of that. I will be with Rita and Kyle and Terry, who are all very responsible people. I promise not to drink and drive. If it would make you feel better, I'd be willing to call you before we leave for home, so that you know exactly when to expect me.

You may honestly believe that none of these precautions is necessary. After all, *you* know that you can be trusted! But you are being honest with your parents by acknowledging that you have heard their concerns. By explaining exactly how you will handle the evening, you are demonstrating just how well you've listened to them. You've stayed away from attacking and blaming your parents. ("Everyone else is going!" "Nobody else's parents are so stupid!" "You never trust me!" "You really don't care about me at all, do you!") By not getting into a fight with your parents, you are giving them the space to say "yes" to you, rather than putting them in a position where they either have to say "no" or lose face. And, assuming you will keep your promises, you are giving them an honest picture of the situation.

Of course, none of this guarantees that your parents will give you the answer you want. But you can probably be certain that yelling, arguing, blaming, or complaining wouldn't get you any closer to what you want.

Here are some other suggestions for open, honest communication:

Stay away from words like "never" and "always." People often feel trapped when they hear these words. "You never listen to me" or "You always ask such stupid questions" are definitely fighting words. "Sometimes you don't listen to me" is a sentence that your parents are more likely to hear. "Sometimes I don't feel that what I say gets through to you. How can we make sure that I know it does?" is even more likely to get through.

Identify the problem rather than the person at fault. As in the previous example, identifying the problem gives both sides room to solve it. "How can we make sure that we're really hearing each other?" opens up space for your parents to ask *themselves* if they've been listening to you carefully enough. Accusing them of "never" listening will probably send them rushing for insults of their own.

Stick to the point. Nothing is more wearing than having someone say, "And why didn't you pick me up at school last Tuesday?" in the middle of a fight about doing the dishes. If the discussion, or argument, or fight, has solving its problem as its goal, then it won't help to bring in an unrelated problem. Bringing up last Tuesday won't do anything but send the other person searching for his or her own sob story.

Stay away from insults. Phrases like, "Only a jerk would do something like that" or "You must be crazy if that's what you think," don't lead to openness and honesty. They lead to more insults and hitting below the belt. Sometimes people feel powerless and want to hurt others in order to prove that they do in fact affect the people around them. If you are feeling this way, take a short break from the argument. Say that you have to go to the bathroom, take a deep breath and count to ten, find some other excuse to leave the room for a moment. Remember that insulting your parents will only give them more room to insult you—or to withdraw from the conversation in order to protect themselves. If you are in an argument with someone who is insulting you, you may find it tempting to sink to the other person's level. Ask yourself what that will accomplish—and keep sticking to the point!

Be sure that you're understanding the other person's point of view correctly—and let the other person know that you understand. One good way of doing this is simply to repeat the other person's position. Be sure, though, that you're genuinely repeating the person's opinion and not taking the chance to slip in a few insults. Compare the following two restatements:

"In other words, you are worried about all the drunk drivers who are likely to be out on a weekend night, and you're concerned that even if I drive defensively, I might not be able to avoid an accident."

"You seem to think that the roads are crawling with drunk drivers at that hour and that I don't know enough to take care of myself, even though I have been driving for the past two years."

Which statement is more likely to leave the other person feeling that his or her position has been heard?

Like anything else, open, honest communication among family members takes practice. It will probably take you a fair amount of time to learn new ways of talking with your family, and it may take time for them to get used to your new approach. You may find that for two or three weeks, you're communicating with your parents in a different, closer, more productive way—and then suddenly you have one of your old out-of-control fights or stormy silences again. Give it time. People often go back and forth between new and old ways when they are learning a different approach to something. The important thing is that you are seeing and acting on new choices that will at the very least help you feel better about yourself and at best can improve relations among everyone in your family.

6

If You Are . . .

A s you know, every family is different, with its own special circumstances. However, some circumstances can be more stressful than others. If you are a member of a family whose parents are divorced, single, adoptive, dying, or recently dead, you may feel that this aspect of your family is particularly difficult for you. You may not know anyone who is in a similar situation, or you may feel that those whose situations appear to be similar have nothing to offer you to help you cope with *your* life.

Feeling "different," "special," or "the only one" is a major part of the teenage years. Part of this feeling is strongly rooted in reality. You *are* a unique person. No one in the world is exactly like you, not even an identical twin brother or sister. You have special qualities that only you can contribute to the world, just as you have special difficulties that only you face.

However, some of this feeling of being different may not be as true in reality as it sometimes seems to you. The teen years are a time of exploration and discovery. You are finding out things about yourself that you never knew before, or you are becoming aware that the qualities you've taken for granted—in yourself or in your family—are really not true of every person or every family. This feeling of discovery may sometimes lead you to feel *more* unusual or alone than you really are. Even if no one in the world is exactly like you, at least there are some people who are similar. Even if no one has had your exact experiences, at least some people have had experiences that allow them to imagine what you might be feeling. And, of course, even people who are very different from you and who have had very different lives can still love you and be open to the unique qualities that you have.

As you read this chapter, try to keep both points of view in mind. The special qualities and experiences that are yours alone are part of your identity. The qualities and experiences that you share with others are part of your being a human being in a world with other human beings. A special challenge of being in a situation that seems "different" is to continue to reach out to others for the support and companionship that you need while not denying or hiding your own experience.

. . . The Child of Parents Who Are Separating or Divorcing

The time before parents separate is a very difficult one for most children. Even if your parents fight all time, seem extremely unhappy, or have withdrawn a great deal from each other or from you, there may still be a part of you that hopes they will get back together. You may endure a fight by saying to yourself, "I don't care what they do, just so they don't get a divorce." You may get through a parent's absence or emotional withdrawal by saying to yourself, "I may not get to talk to Dad much, but at least he's still here." When your parents finally announce that they are separating or divorcing, it can seem like a terrible blow.

Many children of divorced parents find it difficult to accept their parents' decision. Here are some of the emotions through which they show that difficulty:

Hope. Even though your parents have made it quite clear that they are separating, you keep hoping that it isn't really true. You might think that, "They didn't really mean it—this will all blow over." You might pick a date or an occasion that you are sure will fix everything: "Dad has got to change his mind by Mom's birthday," "Mom can't possibly leave after she sees what a nice Christmas we'll have." Even after one or the other parent leaves, you may hope that the person's mind will change, that someone will have a miraculous new outlook that will save the marriage.

Fear. Once the decision is made, you start to imagine all the consequences that might occur. Will there be enough money in the house? Will one parent or both be extremely unhappy? Will you become responsible for parents or brothers and sisters—"the new man of the house," "the little mother?" Will you have to move? How will your friends react? You may also become fearful about your future. Does this mean that love and marriage are inevitably dead ends? Are you, too, doomed to a "broken" marriage? Can you ever trust someone not to leave you, the way your parent seems to be leaving you now? You may be conscious of these fears or you may just feel a general sense of panic and uncertainty. What will the future bring?

Blame. Some people cope with a difficult situation by looking for someone to blame. It's natural to feel anger at your parents for taking an action that you have no control over but that nevertheless has a major effect on your life. Some people translate that anger into blame, focusing on events or personality traits that they believe have "caused" the divorce. "If Dad weren't so lazy, he'd earn more money and there wouldn't be this problem." "If Mom were more patient, she'd make it easier on Dad and they'd still be together." You might find yourself blaming one parent, both parents, grandparents and other relatives, your brothers and sisters, or even yourself. "If only I hadn't asked for a raise in my allowance . . ." "If only I had been more cheerful when I came home from school . . ." "I don't even know what I did, but I know this is my fault . . ."

Relief. You may have been wishing hard that your parents would stop fighting and start loving each other like the families on television or in books. But once they have announced their decision to separate, you may find yourself ready to face the reality that the marriage is not going to spontaneously "improve" and even feel a certain relief in the decision. Now you don't have to come home each day wondering what the mood of the house is going to be. Now you won't have to wonder where to go to get away from the sound of fighting. Along with fear, anger, and sadness at the changes that are happening, you may feel relieved that you can begin to cope with a new, more promising situation instead of feeling frustrated and helpless.

Guilt. If you do feel relief—or if you feel anger at one or both parents—you may also feel a certain amount of guilt. How can you be glad about this situation when your mother or father is so upset? How can you be looking forward to moving when your little brother is so miserable about it? How can you be so angry at your mother for messing up your life when she's so unhappy already? How can you hate your father when you know that he loves you?

All of these reactions, separately or mixed up together, are natural to children of parents who are separating. Sometimes different family members "split up" these feelings among themselves. You may be acting the "good" child, understanding and helpful, while your younger brother is being angry and your younger sister is being quiet and withdrawn. Each of you may experience a mixture of feelings while acting only one of them out. You may even believe that you can't get angry, be- cause someone else is already doing that, or ask yourself, "What's the use of trying to help out?" when your older sister already seems to have taken over that role.

The first thing to remember is that it's very important to be conscious of whatever feelings you have. It may be painful to face this situation, but the sooner you can face both the separa- tion and *all* your feelings about it, the sooner you can sort things out. Feelings that you bury now will come back to demand your attention at another time. It's natural to "shut down" a little in difficult situations—that's how we cope with pain. But to the extent that you can find ways of expressing your feelings—at least to yourself—you will find yourself ready to accept the situation and make the best of it, even if you don't like it and don't agree with your parents' choices.

Another way to cope with this situation is to reach out. For many people, the times when they could most benefit from reaching out are the times when they least feel like doing so. You may be feeling ashamed that your parents couldn't "make their marriage work," or ashamed that you aren't handling the situation better. You may feel that no one understands your problem—or that everyone understands it—but since it's no big deal to them, why should you be upset? You may not like others to see you when you are sad, angry, or frightened, or you may not trust others to care for you.

These feelings are natural, especially in times of crisis. If you can get past these feelings and give others a chance to support you, you may find that you are better able to face whatever the situation brings. At bottom, you are in a difficult position: Your parents have the power to make a decision that affects your whole life, and you are powerless to affect that decision. Once you can accept this unpleasant reality, you can go on to see how you can best get through it. Reach out to your parents, your brothers and sisters, to other relatives. Ask for the support you need. To calm your fears, ask your parents the specific questions that you want answered: Will we have to move? How will our finances be affected? When will I see the other parent? You can also ask for the emotional support you need. Let your parents know that you want time alone with them, or time to be reassured that they still care for you, even though they are leaving each other. Be aware that your brothers and sisters are going through a difficult time along with you and see how you can help each other through it. It might be most helpful to reach out to people outside the family—other relatives, friends, adults whom you trust, even a support group—to remind yourself that you have a life of your own that is not completely limited to your two parents.

. . . The Child of Parents Who Are Already Divorced

All families have their own special difficulties as well as their special benefits. Families where the parents are divorced may face one or more of the following situations:

- changing arrangements for custody
- financial changes resulting from the divorce
- conflict with relatives of one or both parents
- one or both parents dating
- one or both parents establishing a new relationship or remarrying
- stepchildren from one or both partners in a marriage, each with separate custody arrangements

Each of these situations has something in common with the divorce itself: Each is caused by a decision that deeply affects your life, but which you are powerless to affect. You can't undo your parents' divorce, nor can you decide that they will not date, remarry, move to another city, or magically begin to get along with the relatives of the other parent.

What you can do is figure out what parts of each situation you *can* affect, and then take effective action to do so.

Custody. In most cases, this decision is made by the parents alone, with little to be heard from the child. Job or housing situations may determine a parent's decision about who lives where. In some cases, parents don't agree about custody and ask the court to make a decision. The court may take the wishes of the children into account but will not necessarily be bound by those wishes. If you are not satisfied with your family's custody arrangements, you can find out what realistically you can change. It may be that, even if you are not living with the parent you would have chosen, you can arrange to spend more time with the other parent. It's possible that you could convince your parents to change the custody arrangement, or at least to try out another plan.

If you are not able to affect the structure of your custody arrangements—or if you are satisfied with your present arrangement—there are still ways in which you can affect your relationship with both parents. When you don't live with a parent, you and that parent may both have to be extra conscious of what you can do to have satisfying time together. Perhaps you are spending a lot of time in activities with your visiting parent, when you would prefer to be part of his or her daily routine. If so, find a way to make that clear to the parent. He or she may not realize that "just being" with him or her is enough for you.

In some cases, especially soon after a divorce, the parent you don't live with has a hard time being with his or her children. They may be reminders of loss, or the parent may have fears of not being able to be a good parent. You may be able to break through to your parent, making it clear that what you most want is contact with him or her. Or you may have to accept a period of withdrawal and difficulty. In either case, try to keep in sight both your own feelings and the other person's situation. Remember that the parent is having problems of his or her own, but don't remember in order to "excuse" his or her behavior; rather you should remind yourself that you are not necessarily the cause of his or her withdrawal. It's all right to be angry if you don't like the way you are being treated. While you are angry, though, it may help to remember that being treated in a way you don't like doesn't mean that something is wrong with *you*.

You may find after a divorce that you are still very angry with one or both parents, and that this anger is affecting your behavior toward them. Even when a parent does reach you, you may find yourself unwilling to "forgive" him or her for what you see as wrongs committed against you. If you feel overwhelmed by anger, depression, or indifference, you may want to find a counselor, a sympathetic adult, or a support group that can help you to vent your feelings and move on. It may help to express those feelings to one or both parents, just to clear the air. It may help to find something specific to ask of that parent—special time together, a chance to talk, an event to share—to remind yourself that this person still cares about you and wants to share your life. Your parent may have been interpreting your anger as a signal that he or she should "back off"; if you want more contact, you might want to ask for it.

Financial Changes. Again, you can't control the basic situation, which will be determined by decisions that your parents make. What you can do, however, is figure out how you can best cope with the situation, and what kind of support you can ask for from your parents and from others in your life.

The first thing you can do about changed financial arrangements is to get information. Ask one or both parents just what the financial situation is. That doesn't necessarily mean that they will tell you their salaries and show you their income tax forms, but they may be able to clarify what they can afford and what they can't.

You may disagree with your parents' perceptions of what's "affordable" or "necessary." Why, you wonder, can your mother afford a new winter coat for your sister but not buy you that leather jacket you've been wanting? How come your father just got a brand-new car and then tells you that he can't afford an extra ten dollars for your big date next week?

Unfortunately, when your parents control the money, they get to make those decisions. They may be able to explain them to you in a way that satisfies you, or they may not choose to do so. Even if they do explain their reasoning ("You have a perfectly good coat, but your sister's was falling apart." "I'm a salesman—I need a new car to impress my customers."), you may not agree with it. What you can do is ask them to be as clear as possible with you about what you can expect in the way of money: a regular allowance, extra money for new clothes, nothing beyond what is absolutely necessary, or a changing situation from month to month depending on outside circumstances. Then, when you know the situation as well as you can, you can decide what you want to do next.

What are your options if you're dissatisfied with your family's money situation? You might consider getting a job, doing odd jobs like baby-sitting or lawn mowing, or reevaluating the way you spend and save the money you do have. You may be able to work out a financial plan for yourself that solves all your money problems—or you may have to accept a little frustration until you are old enough to be financially self-sufficient. Either way, learning how to handle your financial situation—whatever it is, whoever is responsible for it—will help you enormously when you do become financially responsible for yourself.

Family Conflict. Even in families that are not divorced, the relatives of one parent may not get along with those of the other. After a divorce, these conflicts may become especially sticky—and you may feel caught in the middle.

Often children in this situation feel uncomfortable out of a sense of torn loyalties. You love Aunt Frieda, but you also love your dad. When she starts in on how badly your dad has treated your mother, you don't know whose side to take. Or you know that you want to take your dad's side, but you don't want Aunt Frieda to get mad at you. Or you agree with Aunt Frieda that your dad acted badly, but it seems wrong to say so.

These torn loyalties are especially painful when they involve your parents, but it may help to remember that you will be facing similar conflicts throughout your life. If you marry or establish a permanent relationship with someone, you will have his or her relatives to deal with, with all the mix of different opinions and loyalties that that involves. As your close friends marry or become involved, you will have their partners to deal with, just as you will have to cope with how your friends receive your boyfriends or girlfriends. Handling the conflicting opinions that people you love have about each other can be difficult, but it can be done!

The main thing to remember is that you have the right to love and be loyal to whomever you choose. No one should expect you to give up one important family relationship in order to maintain another. If this happens, or if you perceive that it is happening, *you* can make the decision to keep *both* relationships, regardless of how anyone else feels about it. Begin by reminding yourself that you have a right to both relationships. If you are clear about refusing to discuss a parent in a way that feels uncomfortable to you, sooner or later, relatives may get tired of trying to draw you into conversations you are uncomfortable with. Even if their behavior doesn't change, your own clarity about your decision might help make the situation more relaxed for you.

What about the case of parents talking about each other with you? Here again you will find it helpful to get clear about how you feel. If your parents are talking about each other in a helpful way, in a way that you feel makes it easier to stay close to both parents, then you will want to continue the conversations. If, however, you feel that you are somehow being disloyal, or that you are being pumped for information, then you will probably want to find a way to stay out of such discussions. If changing the subject doesn't work or doesn't feel comfortable, explain to each parent that you want to stay close to both of them and that the best way for you to do that is not to discuss them with each other. It's usually most effective to explain this without accusations or blame: Avoid putting either parent in the wrong. ("I don't believe you're asking me about my dad—don't you know that I love him, too!" "It's pretty low of you to try to find out about Mom through me.") Instead, focus on what you want and what you are and are not willing to do.

Here again, you may find yourself having to stick to your position after repeated attempts by your parents to change your mind. If your family has had a pattern of indirect communications—where people talk to someone other than the person they're having the problem with—this pattern will not change just because there has been a divorce. If *you* want to change this pattern, be prepared to stay focused and clear about what you want, even if it seems to upset your parents. Find other ways of supporting and comforting your parents, ways that do not put you in the position of having to give up a relationship with either one.

Parents Dating or Remarrying. This issue is difficult for children of all ages, even children whose parents divorce or remarry when the children are already married themselves. It's particularly difficult, though, when you yourself are just beginning to date and develop romantic relationships.

As with all these issues, it's helpful to try to sort out what your problem is and what you can reasonably request of your parents as a change. It also may be helpful to share *all* your feelings, even the "unreasonable" ones, either with your parents or with a friends or another adult. One part of you may understand that your mother has a right to date; meanwhile, part of you is furious that she's playing any role except that of your mother. You have a right to those feelings, and your mother has a right to date. If you can both discuss this openly, it might clear the air. In any case, find a way to acknowledge all of your feelings, whether they're pleasant or not. Hiding your feelings from yourself only means that they will come back in some other way.

Once you've accepted this new situation and vented your feelings in some way, you may want to talk to your parents about what you can expect and what you'd like. You may *wish* they'd stop dating altogether, which they probably won't do. (Even if they did, would you really be happy making such a restrictive request on your parents and living with the consequences of their depriving themselves to that extent?) However, you may be reassured if they introduce you to their dates, or if they include you in some of their social life. Or perhaps they have been trying to include you and you'd rather be left out until the relationship becomes serious. You may miss eating dinner with them, or wish for some special time just for you and your parent, which you might request. Try approaching a conversation with your parents as though both of you could get what you want—you may come up with some new ways of handling the situation that feel good to both of you.

Likewise, if your parents remarry, you may not be consulted about this decision. But you can decide what points you can affect about your new living situation. Even if you don't keep your own room by yourself, is there some way to protect your privacy, such as your own closet or locked desk? If the new adult in the household has his or her own rules, can you discuss these rules and come up with a reasonable compromise? Once you decide to accept this new situation, what are the possibilities for working within it to create the kind of family relationships you'd like?

One final word: No one has the right to seriously intrude upon your physical privacy, to abuse you, or to threaten you. If you feel that any adult in your life—parent, stepparent, or any other relative—is abusing or threatening you, it is *not* disloyal to discuss this with another adult, inside or outside the family. You have the right to protect yourself, your body, and your privacy in any way you can.

. . . The Child of a Dead or Dying Parent

If one of your parents is dead or dying, you are facing one of the most difficult situations you will ever have to face. What you learn from this situation will be a resource for you for the rest of your life.

A parent's death can lead to several conflicting feelings. Different people respond to this event in different ways. None of your feelings are "right" or "wrong"—they just *are*.

Here are some of the feelings that you might be experiencing:

Anger. You may find yourself angry at aspects of how the death was handled by other adults. "Why wasn't I told the truth sooner?" "Why didn't the doctor do something else?" "Why did my dad decide not to have that last operation?" Or you may resent the parent who is ill or dead for not having taken better care of himself or herself. "She shouldn't have been driving on such a rainy night." "He shouldn't have smoked so much." You may find yourself blaming another person for your parent's death, particularly if your parent was killed in a traffic accident.

All of these reactions have their own validity. At bottom, though, they're covering up an anger about something much deeper: Something is happening that greatly affects your life and yet you are powerless to do anything about it. If you had the power to keep your parent alive, you wouldn't need to be angry, you could simply exercise that power. Since you can't change the fact of your parent's death or illness, you may try to deal with the pain and frustration by getting angry.

Guilt. If you've ever been angry with the dead or dying parent, or if you've ever neglected this parent or behaved less than perfectly with him or her, you may be feeling guilty now. In fact, no one behaves perfectly toward another human being and everyone gets angry at loved ones. It's part of being human. You may also feel guilty for ever feeling happy or excited about something, even if a parent is dead or dying.

Numbness. The whole death or illness may simply seem unreal to you. You may not be able to believe that your parent is really dying, or is really gone and is not coming back. You may find yourself immersed in fantasies about your parent being well or alive again, or simply feel numb and indifferent about everything in your life.

All of these responses—anger, guilt, and numbness—are ways of protecting yourself against the huge pain and loss of losing someone whom you love very much. It is difficult to face that pain. When you are ready to do so, you can find a way to grieve for your parent, rather than covering up your grief with other feelings.

If your parent is still alive, you might try shifting the focus of your attention from your anger, guilt, or numbness to really making the most of the time you have left. Rather than looking for what you or the other person didn't do, should have done, or could have done, look at what you can still do.

If your parent is dead and you are still actively grieving for him or her, allow yourself to feel the loss. You might also allow yourself to feel the presence of this person in your thoughts, your feelings, and your actions. It can be painful to be reminded of a person who is dead, but it can also be comforting, letting you know that although your parent is dead, he or she lives on in your life.

. . . The Child of Adoptive or Foster Parents

Children of adoptive or foster parents know firsthand how important it is to be flexible in human relations. Love, caring, and family take many different forms; fortunately, human beings have been flexible enough to recognize these many forms and make the most of them.

Some children of adoptive or foster parents are concerned about making contact with their birth parents. This is happening more and more often these days, as the old ideas about "protecting" adoptive and birth parents from one another are breaking down. If you are interested in finding your birth parents, you may be able to do so through various agencies that have sprung up to assist adopted children.

In such cases, children may feel guilty about wanting to get to know their birth parents. They may worry about hurting the feelings of their adoptive parents, about seeming ungrateful, or about losing their closeness with their adoptive parents. This is a complicated issue, but, as with children of divorce, it is your right to seek closeness with *all* the members of your family if you wish to. You may need to wait until you have reached age 18 or 21, depending on the laws in your state and on the wishes of your adoptive parents. You may also want to make sure that your adoptive parents understand that you are not interested in your birth parents because of any dissatisfaction with the love and care you received from your adoptive parents. Your adoptive parents will decide for themselves how they want to handle this issue, but at least you can be clear about your end of the communication.

You may also ask yourself your purpose in seeking your birth parents. Do you have the fantasy that there are "ideal" parents out there somewhere, with none of the "flaws" that you perceive in the people you live with? Are you hoping that troubling questions of your own identity—What do you want to do with your life? What values are important to you?—will magically be solved just by finding people to whom you're biologically related? Any frustrations or dissatisfactions you currently feel will not be dissolved by meeting another person or two, even if those people turn out to become important people in your life.

As you face your special situation, whatever it is, remember that your identity is shaped as much by the struggles you undergo as it is by the love and nurturing that you receive. Coping with your situation can prove to be a rich resource for you as you go on to shape the rest of your life.

7

In Times of Trouble

All families face different types of trouble at some time in
their lives. The trouble may be caused by the crisis of one
particular member—an accident, an unexpected pregnancy, an
unfortunate incident that leads to jail or detention of some
kind. A member of the family may be seriously ill, or die unex-
pectedly. An adult might lose a job, or be seriously affected by a
death or illness of a relative.

Or perhaps the family trouble is in the form of an ongoing
problem—someone permanently out of work, a chronic
shortage of money, an aging parent or relative requiring a lot of
care, a child who seems to have perpetual difficulty in school or
socially. And there are some conditions that are not actually
"trouble," but may be perceived that way by some families. For
example, many families include a member who is handicapped
in some way—blind, deaf, physically impaired, or mentally
retarded. This is not necessarily "trouble" but more like a
particular characteristic of that family. However, many families
relate to this condition as "their special problem."

Think about the families you know. Is there any family you
can think of that hasn't had some trouble at some time? Even if it
seems to you that there are some happy families who simply

sail through life, you might be surprised to discover the problems that these families have that you never hear about. Different families face their problems in different ways, but you can be sure that any family will have some kind of trouble at some point.

While it is true that all families face difficulties, not all families do so in the same way. Some families are definitely better than others when it comes to handling crises or problems, or when it comes to the adults helping the teens and children make it through the difficulties.

What seems to be most important in family response to crises is openness and honesty. The families that have the easiest time facing a hard situation are the ones that can agree openly that there is a problem and that all the family members have painful or angry feelings about it. For example, if a parent loses a job and the family faces severe financial problems, this is a difficulty. But it is a difficulty that can be made somewhat easier by the parents explaining to the children what is going on and conveying to the children that, while it is frightening to be short of money, the parents are prepared to deal with the problem. The parents are able to admit that they are worried, short-tempered, or anxious, rather than pretend that "nothing is wrong" and then blow up inexplicably at their children.

Let's look at the different ways a family might handle a situation where, for example, the mother has lost her job and the family's income is in trouble. The mother, after a long day of job-hunting, comes home discouraged and upset. Unfortunately, that's the moment that the teenager picks to ask for his or her carfare or gas money to get to school. The mother, at the end of her rope, blows up, shouting, "I don't know what you do with all the money I give you! Do you think I'm made of money?"

This is the kind of incident that might happen in any family. But think of all the different ways in which a family might handle this incident afterwards:

The mother could simply not say anything about it afterwards. When the teenager brings up the fight, the mother says, "Let's just not talk about it." The teenager, then, doesn't know how serious the money problem is or what he or she could do to help.

The mother could say, "I'm sorry I lost my temper." When the teenager asks if there is a problem with money, the mother could say, "There's no problem at all. What do you mean? I just lost my temper." This response might make the teen feel even worse. The teen can tell that there *is* a problem, so it is very confusing to have the mother say that there isn't one.

The mother could say, "You have to be more careful with money! If you didn't spend so much, we wouldn't be in so much trouble. What about that new sweater you just bought? If you hadn't bought that sweater, you'd have all the money you need." The mother may be speaking out of her own genuine fears about the family finances. And there really might not have been enough money for the teen to buy a new sweater. But by blaming the teenager, the mother is making it seem as though the teen is the one responsible for all the family problems and that the teen has the power to fix these problems by not being so extravagant. By waiting until after the fact to tell the teen what to do, the mother really isn't giving the teen a chance to help. And it really isn't true that the teen is responsible for *all* the family problems. The teen knows this—but feels bad anyway. And besides feeling bad, he or she feels confused. How can the mother believe something that isn't true?

The mother could say, "I'm sorry I lost my temper. You know I've been worried about money. I just took those worries out on you." Then she and the teen could go on to figure out some things the teen could actually do to help:

- Are there some places where the teen could help cut back on spending?
- Is there a realistic way the teen could earn some money, even if just his or her own spending money?
- Maybe the teen and mother can agree that right after the mother gets home from job-hunting is not a good time for the teen to mention any problem. They can agree to save problems for after supper, when the mother is more rested and relaxed.

By acknowledging that there is a problem and coming up with concrete ways in which the teen can help, the family has not *solved* the difficulty. There is still not enough money. The mother is still worried about money. The teenager may still feel frightened, angry, or upset about not being able to buy everything he or she wants, or about knowing that the mother is unhappy. But the problem is out in the open. It isn't being blamed on anyone, and the teen is not being shut out of it. At least the bad feelings have a place, instead of being hidden away out of sight. The problem with hiding bad feelings away is that they don't really *go* away. They only cause guilt and shame, and because they are hidden, they often come to seem even bigger than they are.

Look over the various ways families have of dealing with trouble. Do any of these seem familiar to you? You may find that your family always deals with trouble in just one way. Or, you may find that, like many families, yours deals with trouble in a mixture of ways. Maybe your family is able to deal with some kinds of trouble openly and honestly, but hides other kinds of trouble out of sight. Or perhaps your parents or the adults in the family each have different styles of dealing with trouble, some of which may be more comfortable for you and others which may be less pleasant. Some families switch: one day, handling things by blaming the children; the next day, pretending that nothing is wrong. This can be the most confusing of all.

Think about the ways in which your family handles trouble. Then think about the different ways *you* feel about problems your family has had or is having. Do you feel:

- angry?
- ashamed?
- worried?
- as if it's your fault?
- as if it's all the fault of one other person?
- confused?
- hopeful?
- as if you don't care, it's not your problem?
- as if you don't care, the problem is not that serious?

You may have all of these feelings, or just one, or some mixture. Or you may have different feelings at different times. The important thing is to start to recognize your feelings and to understand the way your family deals with problems. Because, no matter what the problem, the following things are likely to be true:

- There is probably something you can do to make yourself feel better.
- You probably can't fix the whole problem all by yourself.
- There are going to be some things you can't do anything about.
- You can't make other people in your family feel better if they don't want to.

For example, in the story about the mother who has lost her job, the teen might feel better by helping out as much as the mother allowed him or her to help. The teen would probably also feel better by figuring out—with or without the mother's help—the good and bad times to talk to the mother. Certainly the teen can't fix the whole problem. Not many teenagers have the power to get their parents jobs, or to give them enough money so that jobs aren't necessary. And even if the teenager weren't costing the parents any money at all, there would still be money problems.

What the teen *can* do is:

- cut down on spending
- earn a little money from babysitting or part-time work
- help out with household work
- be sensitive to the parent's feelings.

What the teen *can't* do is:

- find the mother a job
- provide the family with enough money
- not have any needs of his or her own.

As long as you are living in your family's house, you have a right to bad moods, times when you want attention, and times when you want to be reassured. You don't have to feel guilty about not being "perfect" or completely "unselfish" just because someone else is having a hard time, too.

If your mother will let you make her feel better, there are probably lots of things you can do to cheer her up or comfort her. But if she cannot get over feeling worried, anxious, or angry, it's not in your power to make her feel better. Let's say she comes home after a day of looking for work and you go to give her a hug and a cheerful "hello." She says, "Get away from me—can't you see I'm tired!" You might feel that if only you had done something else when she got home, then she would be in a good mood. But the point is, she's an adult. If she wants you to do something specific, she can tell you. If, whatever you do, she's upset, that's her problem (even though you may feel sad or angry that you can't make her feel better).

One of the best things you can do for yourself in times of trouble is to separate your feelings from the situation. First look at the situation and try to judge it realistically. *Then* look at all the different feelings you are having about it. When you know both what is happening and how you feel about it, you can decide what you can do, what you want to do, and what you have no control over. This may not solve the problem. If you are feeling sad, angry, or frightened, you will probably continue to have at least some of those feelings for a while. After all, life has sad, upsetting, and scary times as well as good and happy times. But by looking clearly at the situation, you at least are not feeling any worse than you absolutely have to feel.

For example, in the case of the teen whose mother has lost her job, the first thing to do is to look at the situation realistically.

What, realistically, is going to change now that the mother is not working? Will the family have to move right away? Will the family have to give up a car, or return furniture or appliances that were brought on the installment plan? Will some members of the family have to go and live with relatives until there is enough money for them to return? Just how bad is it going to get—and how bad is it not going to get?

Also realistically, how long is it going to take for the mother to find another job? Do you know anyone else whose parent lost a job? How long was that person out of work? Is that person's situation the same as your mother's, or is there something different about it?

Both of these types of question are hard for a teen to answer by himself or herself. That's why it's good for the family to handle things openly. Perhaps the mother has already explained everything: "I have an announcement to make. I've lost my job. They were laying people off indefinitely, so I'm not sure whether I can get that job back. But I think that, in a month or so, I can find another one. In the meantime, we'll still have some money coming in from unemployment and some savings, so you are not to worry about money. We'll have to cut back on some things, like new clothes and trips to the movies, but you kids will still get a small allowance, and we won't starve. Times may be a little bit harder than before, but we'll all work together and we can handle it."

By explaining the problem and her response to it, the mother is explaining just how serious the situation is—and how serious it is not. If your parents deal with a crisis in this way, you may already have all the information you need to understand the situation. And, of course, you don't need to know everything your parents know about it; you just need to know what you can expect.

If your parents are not this open about a particular kind of trouble in your family, and if you feel uneasy or upset about the problem, you might want to try to find out more. Perhaps your parents don't realize that you are aware of the problem and concerned about it. In that case, you may only need to ask your parents to tell you what's going on. If something in particular is bothering you ("Will we have to move?" "Does this mean you'll never get another job?"), ask about it. Your parents may be happy to give you the information once they realize that you already know there's a problem.

Perhaps, though, your parents refuse to talk about the problem. They may get very upset when you bring it up. They may want you to "pretend" that there is no problem. ("You didn't want that new jacket anyway, did you?") They may blame you for the problem when you bring it up. ("If you didn't spend so much, there wouldn't be any problem about money!") They may become angry and start blaming someone else, either in your family ("Your stupid mother! She never could keep a job!") or outside your family ("If Grandpa Jake would help out, there wouldn't be any problem!"). You may find this "blaming" upsetting, both because you care about the person being blamed and because you suspect that the blaming isn't the whole truth. (How could your mother help it that she was laid off? Is it Grandpa Jake's fault that she lost her job? Could he really afford to support your whole family?) Even if what your parents say is technically true (You *could* cut down on your own spending. Grandpa Jake is rich and *could* help out. Your mother *was* late to work every day for a week.) it doesn't answer your question. And it doesn't solve the problem. You are probably less interested in knowing whom to be angry at than in knowing how bad the situation is and in figuring out what you can do about it.

If, therefore, you feel that your parents' responses aren't very helpful, you might want to find out the information in another way. Perhaps by observing them and what actually happens, you can see that, while there is less money for luxuries, your mother still came up with the money to buy you a scarf for your birthday—so you're probably not completely at the end of your funds. If you know other people who have lost their jobs, or if someone in your family has lost a job before, you might be able to get a realistic perspective, even if your parents aren't helping you to do so.

If you feel that you are still confused about your situation, or if the picture you have of it is a very frightening or upsetting one—maybe you imagine that you will soon be moving to another state, like the family down the street did when their dad lost his job—you might try to check out the situation with another adult. Perhaps a relative will be more honest or more helpful than your parents have been able to manage. A teacher, school counselor, social service agency, or adult friend might be able to set you straight. Even if you find out something upsetting, at least you won't have to live in fear. You'll know what the problem is—and then you can face it.

Once you've gotten the clearest picture of the situation that you can, you are ready to look at your own feelings about it. Remember that the more honestly you can face your own feelings, the better you will be able to handle the situation. If, for example, your mother is out of work, one of your feelings may be anger. You are mad that your mother didn't keep her job, which means that you can't buy some things that you want. Perhaps this feeling makes you feel guilty. You think, "How can I be worried about my new jacket at a time when my mother is so upset about more important things?" You think you *shouldn't* be angry, so you try to pretend you're not.

Unfortunately, this doesn't work. If you feel anger, you feel anger. And if it doesn't come out one way, it will come out another. Maybe you'll find some "good" reason to get angry at your mother, because you aren't comfortable to be angry at her for a "bad" reason. It's "not OK" to be mad because she lost her job, but is it "OK" to be mad at her for being late to pick you up after school? Or for not listening while you tell her a story? The anger hasn't gone away, it's just found a different excuse. The problem is that, if the anger is being let out for some other reason than the real one, it won't make you feel better to express it. Getting angry at your mother because she didn't pick you up on time will just leave you feeling more guilty and confused than before—if that's not what you're really mad about.

Or perhaps the anger will be directed at another person than your mother. Perhaps you'll be mad at your father, who should be earning enough money so that your mother's job loss is not a problem. Or at your teacher, who is so unreasonable that she expects you to do your homework even though things are so bad at home. Again, this kind of anger won't make you feel any better, and it might even alienate someone that you would rather be close to.

The worst thing you can do with your "hidden" anger (or with any other hidden feeling) is to take it out on yourself. Being depressed for a long period of time—feeling like nothing in life is worthwhile or feeling like you are a worthless person—is often a way of covering up deep feelings of anger against someone. Because you don't feel safe being angry at the person, you try not to have any feelings at all. Or you get angry at yourself: "Why am I so ugly? Why am I so dumb? What's wrong with me, anyway?" Sometimes teens in these moods drink too much, do drugs they don't want to do, or have sexual relationships they don't really want, just because they don't know what else to do with their real feelings.

So it's very important to identify all the feelings you may have about your family's trouble, whether these feelings seem "good" or "right" or "wrong" or "bad" to you. You don't necessarily have to *express* your feelings. Maybe your family is having difficulty with an aging relative who is living with you. You may sometimes feel like, "I wish Uncle Sol would just die so we wouldn't have to put up with him any more." You need to know you feel this way, but you don't need to tell Uncle Sol! Or your parents, or any other family member. You may want to write out your feelings, promising yourself that you will hide or even burn the paper afterwards. You may be surprised at how much better you feel being honest with yourself. Some people enjoy drawing pictures of their feelings, or of the way they see a situation. Drawing Uncle Sol as a big monster swallowing up your house might help you to get those frustrated feelings out into the open and then you can bring your good feelings into the open, too.

Here are some situations in which you might want to write out, draw, or just think about all your feelings:

- divorce
- someone going back to work after you've been used to having him or her at home
- death
- someone's illness
- someone getting old

- a brother or sister having a problem such as an unwanted pregnancy, trouble with the law, or a crisis requiring institutionalization
- your having a problem like that
- having to leave one household and go to live in another
- someone who lives with you and has a problem with drinking, drugs, gambling, or some other type of addiction

If the problem is an ongoing one, you've probably been having feelings about it for a long time. In the case of a sudden problem—a death or serious accident or the news of a divorce—you might find yourself going through some of the following three stages.

In the first stage, you may feel so shocked at the bad news, that you can't quite believe it is happening. This refusal to believe is called *denial*. When people get bad news, they often try to find a way to deny that it is true. Or they may try to deny their own painful feelings about it.

How do people deny bad news or tragedies? Sometimes, by pretending it doesn't really matter. "Mom and Dad were going to get divorced sooner or later, anyway." "Most people have job troubles—I don't think our family's problems are so different." "I didn't really like living in our old house anyway." These statements may be perfectly true. But they may be *both* true *and* a way of trying to handle the feelings of sadness, anger, or fear that go along with the truth.

Sometimes, people deny bad news by trying to place blame. "If Mom really loved me, she wouldn't be going back to work." "If only Grandma had stopped smoking, I bet she'd still be alive." Again, there may be some truth in some of these statements—or there may be no truth at all. Either way, the blaming is a way of trying to avoid the real feelings. Even if you know where to put the blame, you're still left with the problem.

And sometimes people try to blame themselves. This may be the most painful choice of all. Now you not only feel sad, but guilty, too. "If only I had been a better kid, I bet my Dad wouldn't have gone away." "I wish I had spent more time with Aunt Rose before she died." "I should have gotten a job; then I bet we'd have more money." If you find yourself trying to blame yourself, you might try putting your blame "on hold." Say to yourself, "I'm not going to think about whether I'm to blame or not. Maybe I am, maybe not. But I'm going to put the blame on hold and try to think about how I really feel."

Here are some other ways in which people deny their feelings or try to avoid them:

- "I wouldn't mind . . . but this is such a bad time."
- "If it had happened last year (or next year), it would have been all right—but now . . ."
- "I don't mind the divorce itself, I just mind that we have to leave our old house (or that we have to stay in our old house, or some other *part* of the problem instead of the whole problem)."
- "I don't mind, but I know Mom (or Dad), or my brother, or someone else—anyone but you!) is having a hard time."
- "I don't mind—but I wonder what my friends (or our relatives, or someone else) are going to say."
- "I don't believe it. Maybe Mom and Dad will change their minds and get back together. (Or, maybe the doctor made a mistake. Or, maybe this is just a dream and I'll wake up.)"

It's perfectly natural to try to avoid painful feelings. And when some crisis happens that shakes up your world, it's natural to try to protect yourself, as most people do, by trying to make it "not happen." If there was something you could *do* to change the situation—save the person's life, get your parents back together, get the person out of trouble—you'd probably do it. If there really isn't anything you can do, you may try to pretend there is, by blaming yourself or by "reasoning" that you really don't care. If you hear yourself saying any of the things that are listed as "denial," you might take a deep breath and be prepared for some more difficult feelings to "hit you" at some point. Or you might try writing, drawing, or talking to someone as a way to express the feelings underneath.

In the second stage, after the denial wears off, you may become angry. Or, in order to hide the anger, you may become depressed. "I don't deserve this terrible problem!" you may be feeling. "This shouldn't happen to me!" Or you may think, "How can Mom and Dad screw me up this way?" Or even, "So-and-so has no *right* to die and make me so unhappy!"

Anger at someone who is causing you pain is a very natural emotion. You may feel angry at someone who is causing you pain even if you know the other person can't help it. It's especially natural to feel angry at someone for dying and leaving you. Your conscious mind may understand that the person is dying because it can't be helped, not because he or she wants to. But you are angry, because you don't want that person to die.

If someone in your family or someone you are close to is very sick or dying, you should expect that your moods will change a lot, and that anger will be part of those moods. Being angry at someone for dying does not mean you are a bad person or don't love the dying person. It means that you *do* love him or her. That's why you are angry. You don't get angry at people you don't care about.

You don't necessarily have to express your anger at the dying person. You might try writing, drawing, or talking it out to someone else. Nor do you have to stay depressed, sad, or withdrawn just to prove how upset you are. You can try to find and enjoy the good moments, either with the dying person or with the other members of your family or circle of friends. Having someone you love die is one of the hardest experiences a human being ever faces. You don't have to expect yourself to handle it "perfectly." You're allowed a mix of feelings and actions, like any other human being.

In the third stage, finally, after your denial and your anger, you can work your way through to a period of acceptance and understanding. Finally, you can come to live with whatever the situation brings, and to face it in the best way you know how.

Accepting a situation doesn't mean you have to like it or agree with it. Maybe you think, after all is said and done, that it really is your mom's fault that she lost her job and you do feel critical of her behavior. You have a right to that opinion, but that's different from wishing hard for her to become a different, more responsible person if that's not really who she is.

Likewise, you may not really believe that a seriously ill person is going to die. You can still hold onto the hope that the person may somehow recover. But you are also able to face the reality that the person may not recover, and you are able to accept whatever way the person has chosen to face his or her death, even if you wish the person would "fight a little harder" or "listen to the doctor more." You feel acceptance *along with* your disagreement.

Just because acceptance is the last stage of the mourning process does not mean that it is somehow "better" than the other two. It may be necessary to deny reality or to deny your own feelings for a time—exactly in order to give yourself time to face a situation. But sooner or later, acceptance is important. If you feel you are having difficulty with any one of these three stages, you might try to find someone with whom to talk about it. A counselor, a support group, or just an understanding friend can help you through this difficult time.

After you have assessed the situation realistically and come to terms with your own feelings about it, then you can ask yourself what you can actually do about it. You might want to make mental or written lists of the following:

- What can I do to change the situation?
- What would I *like* to do to change the situation? (For example, if the situation is that your mother is out of work, perhaps what you *can* do is get a babysitting job. What you would *like* to do might include earning enough money for the whole family, even though you know you can't actually do this.)
- What can I do to feel better about the situation?
- What can I do to help other people in my family feel better about the situation?
- What isn't going to change, no matter what I do?

It's important not to feel responsible, either for the situation or for other people's feelings about it. You may be able to help other people to feel better—or you may not. It depends somewhat on you, but mainly on the other person.

Likewise, it's important not to feel completely helpless. There's always *something* you can do, even if it's only to figure out a way to get your mind off your problems, or to give yourself a quiet time to feel sad every day. Just because you can't make the situation all better doesn't mean that you are helpless. Just because you feel sad, or angry, or afraid doesn't mean you will always feel that way or that you have done something wrong.

It takes years to learn the difference between what you can and can't change—and there's no one right answer to that question, ever. As you start learning to assess a situation and to accept your own feelings about it, you will be gaining valuable skills, courage, and wisdom that will support you throughout your whole life.

8

When Problems Can't Be Solved at Home

Some families have a family code that says: "We take care of our own problems. We don't talk to outsiders." These families believe that there is something shameful about going outside the family to get help with a problem, or even to admit to any "outsider" that a problem exists. Your parents may convey this message to you in subtle ways. "What did you tell *him* for?" a parent might say. Or he or she might simply get very quiet or very annoyed when you remark that someone was asking how everything was. Either way, you get the message: Don't talk about this. Or your parents may give you direct instruction: "You are not to tell any of your friends that your mother has lost her job. We don't want to bring shame on the family."

While many families do hold this belief, many other people believe that there are real problems with this approach. What it actually does is help you to feel ashamed and frightened, and perhaps guilty if you have "accidentally" let someone at school know that you are, say, short of money this week. ("Maybe they'll figure out that my mom's out of work.") It also makes you feel very much alone. If your parents won't give you the answers or the help you need, and if you aren't allowed even to let anyone else know about your situation, you're really stuck.

You're being told, "If we, your parents, can't be perfect, you'll just have to suffer, because there's nobody else in the whole world you can get help or information from but us."

You don't have to accept this message. If you can get the help and information you need from your parents, great. Even then, it is often helpful to have a friend—your own age, an adult, or both—outside of the family talk to, just to get another perspective, or to tell about the feelings that you don't want to share with your own family. You may not want to tell your mom how upset you are that you can't buy that new jacket that you want, but you do feel comfortable complaining to a friend, because you know your friend won't feel as upset as your mother by your complaints. By telling you not to tell anyone else outside the family about your problems, your family is keeping you from getting that help and comfort. You don't have to go along with that if you don't want to.

And, if you are *not* getting the help and information that you need from your family, you definitely should *not* go along with it. Find *someone* you can trust and get what you need. You might choose a counselor or adult friend whom you can trust not to tell your parents, so that you don't have to confront your parents with your difference of opinion. Or you may want to say openly, "I'm not going to pretend about this." Either way, don't let your parents' idea of secrecy keep you from getting what you need.

Some things families may be ashamed of and ask you to hide:

- Someone in the family is retarded or handicapped. (Some people still believe this is "shameful," even though most people have come to understand that everybody has some kind of "handicap" and some kind of strength. Some are just more visible than others.)
- Someone in the family has had trouble with the law. (Again, while this may be upsetting or painful, it's nothing to be ashamed of.)
- Someone in the family has some kind of mental illness, or is receiving counseling or treatment of some kind. (Before we knew so much about how the mind works, mental ill-

ness was very frightening to many people. And some people, out of ignorance, lumped all kinds of counseling together, from seeing a counselor once a week through living in an institution. Out of fear, some people decided that all emotional problems were shameful, but this was just a way of expressing their fears.)

Someone in the family has a problem with drinking, drugs, or some other addiction. (This may be a difficult problem for the family to solve, but that's no reason to pretend that "nothing's wrong." The problem won't get any better if everyone acts like it isn't there.)

Some people in whom you may choose to confide or get help from about these problems:

- a friend your own age
- another adult in the family
- an adult friend
- a teacher
- a school counselor
- a local mental health service or counseling center
- a social work agency
- Alateen, Nar-A-Teen, Gamblers Anonymous, or one of the other "Anonymous" groups (See the directory in the back of the book.)

If You Are Being Abused

Being "abused" is not the same as just being treated in a way that you don't like or don't think is fair. Being abused is being treated in a way that endangers you physically, mentally, or emotionally. Being abused is being physically harmed by an adult, or being subjected to extreme or unusual punishments, or being touched or related to sexually by a relative or by any adult with whom you don't choose to have a sexual relationship.

It may be difficult to say to yourself that you are actually being abused. If you are being physically abused, for example, you might believe that in some way you "deserve" the punishment, or that your parents or guardians have the "right" to treat you any way they please. But on some level, you probably know that something is wrong. "If it feels wrong, it's wrong," Dr. Sorter says. Being grounded for a week may be an unpleasant punishment that you dislike or don't agree with. But it's not the same as being physically abused or threatened with physical abuse.

It's hard to think about physical abuse as it is an unpleasant and often frightening subject. But if you are in the position of being abused by an adult, you have the right to protect yourself. And the first way to protect yourself is to understand that the following kinds of punishment should definitely be out of bounds:

- violent hitting, especially in any sensitive body area (An occasional slap, while it may not be the best type of punishment, is not necessarily abuse. You should go by your gut feeling; if you feel frightened, or in danger, then it's abuse.)
- burning
- tying someone up or locking someone up
- scratching
- pushing or shoving a child or teen, so that bruises or cuts result
- throwing things
- pushing someone down stairs

Likewise, repeatedly denying a child food, or refusing to buy a child appropriate clothing, can be considered abuse or neglect. "Refusing to buy appropriate clothing" doesn't mean not providing the latest fashions; it means not buying a winter coat or forcing a child to wear worn-out, ragged clothing that is markedly inappropriate.

Sometimes an adult will lose his or her temper, and express himself or herself in physical ways. And some parents have strict rules about sending children away during dinner if the children aren't behaving properly. If your parents punish you in those ways and you still feel comfortable with them, you are probably not being abused—though you may hate the punishments your parents have chosen. But if you feel that you are constantly frightened of your parents, or are aware that there is a major discrepancy between the way they treat you and the way your friends' parents treat them, you may be being abused. Again, you can probably tell by knowing that something feels "wrong" to you.

If you think you are being abused, or if you wonder whether you are, find someone outside your immediate family to talk to. An abusive situation can be very confusing. You may also have evidence from your parents that they love you and care for you, along with treating you so badly. Even if your parents don't show their love, you may believe that, deep down, they really do care about you. You may think that you understand why your parents act the way they do, either because you believe you have misbehaved or because you are sympathetic to the pressures you believe your parents to be under. All of your perceptions and opinions may be absolutely true, but that doesn't change the fact that you deserve to be treated well and *you don't deserve to be abused*. If your parents love you, they will eventually be glad that you helped them find a way to stop treating you badly.

Sexual abuse can be even more complicated. Many teens who have sexual contact with adults, especially adult relatives, find themselves very confused. On the one hand, they don't feel right about the contact. They may be in physical pain as a result of it, or they simply may not like the invasion of their privacy. On the other hand, they may have warm, loving feelings toward the adult, hoping for nonsexual love and affection. They may also feel sexually aroused, even if they are uncomfortable about having a sexual relationship. Adults who are sexually abusing children and teens may tell the child, "This is all your fault. You got me excited." Or, "I can tell that you really want this. You like it, don't you?"

It's important for you to know that you can have these mixed feelings and still not be responsible for the sexual contact. You don't have to do anything you don't feel right about and you are *not* responsible for an adult's misbehavior, no matter what the adult says. Even if you are actively trying to pursue an adult sexually, the adult should be able to help both of you set appropriate boundaries, especially if the adult is a relative or family friend. What is more likely is that the adult has started a sexual relationship and is playing on your feelings of guilt and confusion to make it hard for you to get free.

Just because your body reacts by becoming aroused does not mean that you want to have sex with an adult. Most people want warmth, affection and love—including hugs and kisses—from an adult in the family. If you want these things from an adult, that *does not* mean that you are encouraging him or her to approach you sexually. Adults are authority figures to most teens. And most teens depend on adults for love and guidance. Any adult who takes advantage of your need for love and your respect for authority to touch you in any way that you don't feel comfortable with, to get you to touch him or her, or to have sexual intercourse with you, is not "just doing what you asked for." That adult is abusing you.

Here are some examples of sexual contact that is inappropriate between adults and teens, especially adults who are part of your family. If this kind of behavior is going on in your family, remember that you are *not* responsible for it, no matter what you have said or done, and that you have the right to get help and put a stop to it.

- long or "wet" kisses (as opposed to "ordinary" parent-child kisses)
- touching someone's genitals or nipples, or someone else touching yours
- spending prolonged amounts of time in an adult's bed, or an adult spending any amount of time in yours
- being undressed in front of a parent of the opposite sex, or a parent of the opposite sex being undressed in front of you. (Most sexual abuse takes place by opposite-sex parents. However, there is also some same-sex abuse, so if you feel uncomfortable with a same-sex parent, this applies to that situation as well.)
- prolonged "wrestling" or tickling
- sexual intercourse

There may be other types of sexual contact that you have had that are not on the list. Again, the measure should be your own feelings. If you are uncomfortable with how a parent is treating you or talking to you, then you should talk to someone outside your immediate family to get a perspective on the situation.

How can you tell if the person you talk to has given you good advice? Again, by the way you feel. If you still feel uncomfortable, the person has not correctly understood your situation. Keep looking until you find somebody else. Your body and your physical privacy are important. You have a right to protect them.

For ideas on how to find someone to talk to, see the directory at the end of the book.

Getting Help

There are many situations throughout life in which people need help. Sometimes that help can come in the form of talking to a friend. Sometimes it comes through a support group. Sometimes it comes through talking to a counselor or therapist. There are many, many forms of help, to fit all the different types of people and situations that come up in life.

The directory at the back of this book will give you some ideas for where to look for help. You can also look in the Yellow Pages of your phone book under Counseling, Mental Health, or Social Services; call an information number for your city, state, or country; ask a teacher, counselor, or adult friend; or ask a teen friend.

You may not be satisfied with the first form of help you find. A talk with your counselor might show you that you'd also like a support group. If you find a therapist, you might not feel comfortable talking to him or her, or you might not believe that he or she understands your problem. Don't be discouraged. Keep looking until you find the kind of help that is right for you.

Here are a few situations in which you might turn to some form of outside help:

- You (or a friend) feel overwhelmed with suicidal feelings.
- You can't stand living at home another minute and are planning to run away, or already have run away.
- You are being physically or sexually abused, or you think you might be abused soon.
- You have an unwanted pregnancy, or you are the father in an unwanted pregnancy.
- You feel extremely depressed and don't see the point in activities that used to make you happy. Instead of finding new activities, you don't feel like doing anything at all. It's even an effort to get out of bed in the mornings. (We all feel like this sometimes, but if it goes on for more than a week or two, you may want help in breaking out of this mood.)
- You are taking more than a month or two to get over breaking up with a girlfriend or boyfriend or losing a good friend.
- Someone close to you has died.
- You continually feel nervous, frightened, or worried about something bad that might happen.
- Someone in your family is seriously depressed, or is given to frequent unreasonable or violent outbursts.
- Someone close to you has a serious problem with drinking, drugs, gambling, or some other kind of addiction.
- You have, or are afraid you might have, a problem with drinking, drugs, gambling, or some other kind of addiction.

All of these are situations that trouble people. Often, attention from an understanding person can make a real difference. Some reasons that people don't get help:

- "I'm better off than lots of people I know." (That may be true. Does that mean you shouldn't be even happier?)
- "My parents wouldn't like it." (You may or may not be right about this. Sometimes parents are relieved and happy to know that their children are getting the help that parents can't give them. But even if your parents *wouldn't* like your

getting help, does that mean you should suffer? You are getting help *for* you, not *against* your parents.)

- "Other people might think it's weird." Well, you don't have to tell anyone. But even if other people do find out, are you going to let other people's opinions stop you from doing something good for yourself?)

- "If I get help, I'm admitting that I'm really no good. I should be able to solve this by myself." (The only thing you're "admitting" by asking for help is that you're just a human being, like everybody else. Most people probably already knew this anyway!)

- "Only crazy people talk about their problems to a counselor." (Some people who talk to counselors are "crazy"—that is, they have severe problems that make them basically unable to function in the world. But many others who are not "crazy"—who function quite well in the world—also seek counseling. Movie stars, politicians, lawyers, doctors, writers, waitresses, police officers, and grocery store clerks, as well as college, high school, and grade school students, talk to counselors, call hot lines, join Alcoholics Anonymous, or get some other kind of help. These people are not "crazy," just human beings with troubles they can't solve by themselves.)

- "It wouldn't do any good. Nobody can help me, anyway. I'm too far gone. And nobody has problems like mine, anyway." (Talking to another person about your problems may be a double-edged sword. On the one hand, you'll probably find out that a lot of other people *do* have problems like yours. It might be hard not to feel "special" or that you have "special problems." On the other hand, you do get the comfort of knowing that you're not alone and that someone else *can* help you.)

There are things to look for and ask yourself about in the person or group that you turn to for help. For instance, do you feel like the person or group understands you and your situation? You may not always agree with the answers you get. You may hear some things that are hard to hear. But if you basically feel that the person or group you are talking to understands your situation, you can find a way to learn from your disagreements—and maybe one or both of you will change your minds.

And, do you feel safe with the person or group that you have come to? You may be frightened at first. The idea of getting help may be upsetting to you, so that at first it is hard to accept advice, comfort, or criticism. You may be hearing things that you would rather not hear. But you should also be feeling like you can trust the person or group that you have chosen, and that it's worth it to work through the bad times in order to get to the good ones. If you don't feel safe, can you bring up your frightened feelings with the person or group? Do you feel that these feelings are heard and respected?

Importantly, does the person you have chosen have the credentials that say he or she is qualified? Does the group you are in have a respected history or affiliation? Some religious, political, or "cult" groups prey on people with troubles. Instead of helping you to solve your problems, they encourage you to give up your independence and become totally involved in a group that makes all your decisions for you.

A qualified person . . .

. . . probably has a degree. An MSW (Master of Social Work), CSW (Certified Social Worker), LSW (Licensed Social Worker), MS (Master of Science), MEd (Master of Education), PhD (Doctor of Philosophy—probably in the field of psychology), or MD (Doctor of Medicine—with a specialty in psychiatry) are the degrees that a qualified person is most likely to have. Don't be afraid to ask your counselor what his or her degrees or credentials are and what experience he or she has had.

. . . may be associated with a respected institution. If the person does not want you to tell others about your contact with him or her, there is probably something wrong. Even if you choose not to discuss your counseling with anyone, you should be able to if you choose. A person who does not have a degree but who leads a support group should definitely be associated with a school, well-known teen center, well-known social service agency, or well-established religious group that is attended by at least some of the adults you know.

. . . will not ask you to cut off contact with all of your family and friends. You may discuss reducing or eliminating contact with some of the people in your life—for example, an abusive parent, or a group of friends that encourages you to do things you don't like. But if you feel your counselor wants you to give all of your time, energy, and money to his or her organization—or even to attend meetings or sessions more often than once or twice a week—be careful. You are trying to become more independent, not to become dependent on a new group.

Loving Home/ Leaving Home

All of us start out in some family or family situation that provides us the foundation for what we learn later in life. Right now your "foundation" may seem to you good, bad, or mixed. You may feel that you and your family get along well, badly, or some of both. You may think that when you grow up, your own family will be very much like the one you grew up in or very different or like in some ways and different in others.

Whatever your feelings about your family, the fact remains that sooner or later, as you grow up, you move out into the world. Even if you continue to live at home, you will begin taking on adult responsibilities of advanced school, work, training, or some other form of supporting or developing yourself. You will form your own adult friendships, love relationships, and family relationships.

No matter how you feel about your family, the fact remains, too, that your family is likely to be important to you for a long time to come. Even after you are no longer living at home or financially dependent, your family relationships will probably live on in your feelings and ideas about how life could or should be.

The better you understand your feelings about your family, the easier it will be to go on and live the life *you* choose, whether this is the same, different, or partly the same as the life your family wants you to lead. The ideas in this book should help you to work out problems with your family, and in your own feelings about your family. But you should take comfort in knowing, too, that as you get older and gain real independence, your perspective changes and your relationship with your family usually becomes less conflicted and more balanced. As your circle of independence widens, you will find more and more ways of giving your family the place in your life that works for you.

9

Where to Find Help

The following organizations will be able to provide you with referrals and advice in dealing with a variety of problems or crises that you may have to deal with.

Abuse

Society for the Prevention of Cruelty to Children
161 William Street, 12th Floor
New York, NY 10003
Provides referrals and counseling to families and children suffering from physical and mental abuse.

Childhelp/International
6463 Independence Avenue
Woodland Hills, CA 91370
1-800-4-A-CHILD (1-800-422-4453)
Childhelp provides crisis counseling information and referrals in situations dealing with child abuse.

Alcohol and Drug Problems

Alcoholics Anonymous World Services
475 Riverside Drive
New York, NY 10115
212-870-3400
Provides free referrals for those seeking recovery from alcohol problems.

Alanon Family Intergroup
200 Park Avenue South, Room 814
New York, NY 10003
212-254-7230 or 212-260-0407
Provides information and referrals for families of alcoholics; including Alateen meetings for teenage members of an alcoholic's family.

Alcohol Abuse Helpline
1-800-676-7574
Provides counseling and referrals to treatment centers or self-help groups such as Alateen, Alanon, or Narcotics Anonymous.

Narcotics Anonymous World Service Office
16155 Wyandotte Street
Van Nuys, CA 91406
818-780-3951
Provides general reference services for those seeking recovery from narcotics addiction.

National Cocaine Hotline
1-800-262-2463
Provides information and help for cocaine users, their friends or families.

Pills Anonymous
130 West 72nd Street
New York, NY 10023

212-874-0700
Self-help group for people with drug dependency problems.

Birth Control/ Family Planning

American College of Obstetricians and Gynecologists
202-638-5577
Provides free brochures describing the latest, most effective methods of birth control.

CHOICE Hotline
215-592-0550
Answers teenagers' questions about birth control, pregnancy, sexually transmitted diseases, and other related topics.

Planned Parenthood Federation of America
810 Seventh Avenue
New York, NY 10019
212-541-7800
Provides information on birth control, sexuality, and family life.

National Abortion Federation Hotline
1-800-772-9100
Answers questions about where you can get a safe abortion.

Divorced or Single Parents

Parents Without Partners
301-588-9354
1-800-637-7974
Provides referrals to more than 1,000 local support groups of this organization throughout the country.

Emotional Problems

National Institutes of Mental Health
301-443-4513
Provides referrals for psychological counseling or therapy available in your area.

Incest

Victims of Incest Can Emerge Survivors (VOICES)
312-327-1500
Provides help for people who have been sexually abused. Volunteers will give referrals to self-help groups, therapists, and agencies in their communities.

Runaways

The National Runaway Switchboard
1-800-621-4000
Children and teenagers who run away from home can receive referrals to hospitals, shelters, and social service agencies in their area. The Switchboard also provides a service where runaways and their families can leave messages for one another. All calls are confidential.

Runaway Hotline
1-800-231-6946 (for U.S., excluding Texas)
1-800-392-3352 (for Texas only)
Provides runaways with referrals to local hospitals, shelters, or social service agencies. Runaways can also send messages back home. All calls are confidential.

Organizations such as *The Federation of Protestant Welfare Agencies, Catholic Charities,* or *The Jewish Board of Family Services* often have local chapters listed in the Yellow Pages telephone directory under "Social Service Organizations." They can provide information and referrals for teenagers or families in trouble.

INDEX